Written, edited and designed by the editorial staff of ORTHO BOOKS.

Coordinating Editor and Manuscript: James K. McNair

Photography: Clyde Childress

Special Consultants: Marge Childress, Jeff Goff, Lenny Meyer, Lou Seibert Pappas and Louis Weingarden

All About Pickling

Contents

New ways with an old idea

An ancient method of food preservation—now a culinary taste treat. The return to home-pickling for pleasure, pride and economy.

The varied colors, shapes and textures of pickles rival flowers for a beautiful, edible bouquet.

The art of pickling predates recorded history. It's roots probably go deep into Chinese culture. We know that laborers on the Great Wall of China ate lunches of salted vegetables. In about 2030 B.C. people from northern India brought the seed of the cucumber to the Tigris Valley and the great pickling race was on.

Cleopatra valued pickles as a secret of beauty and health. She introduced them to Julius Caesar and soon he added pickles to the daily diets of the Roman legions and gladiators, thinking pickles would help keep the men in top physical condition.

The pickle passion spread throughout Europe. Queen Elizabeth I was a great pickle fancier. Napoleon esteemed them for their contribution to health.

Pickle influence then spread westward. Early explorers carried kegs of sauerkraut and pickles which they thought would prevent scurvy, a disease caused by vitamin C deficiency. Captain Cook's men rejected his efforts to get them to eat sauerkraut, so he turned it into a status symbol by serving it at the captain's table and in the officer's mess. Soon sauerkraut was so popular with the sailors that it had to be rationed. The "new world" was even named after a Spanish pickle dealer "Americus Vespucius."

Pickles were important in the American colonies as a major method of food preservation. Early Puritan settlers believed that pickles should be served daily as a "sour" reminder to be thankful for the "sweet" gifts of the land.

Thomas Jefferson wrote, "On a hot day in Virginia I know of nothing more comforting than a fine spiced pickle, brought up trout-like from the sparkling depths of that aromatic jar, below the stairs in Aunt Sally's cellar."

Folk medicine cited sour pickles as an aid in balancing the acid-alkaline content of the body and destruction of digestive tract bacteria. Similar beliefs valued the acid in pickle brining solutions for its potassium supply which is important in the assimilation of food.

Early Pennsylvania Dutch meals supposedly contained "seven sweets and seven sours." Pickle patches were important on Southern colonial plantations. The pioneers of the west treasured pickles as the only juicy, green, succulent food available much of the year.

During the Civil War at the battle of Chambersburg, the winning Confederate General Harmon demanded 25 barrels of sauerkraut from the townspeople to help cure his men of scurvy. And General Ulysses S. Grant frequently breakfasted on a cup of coffee and a sliced cucumber in vinegar.

Through the years American homemakers have developed countless recipes for "putting down" pickles in great crocks or "putting up" pickles in glass jars.

Today Americans enjoy pickles more than any previous civilization. Pickle Packers International, Inc. reports that pickles are our number one vegetable in both quantity consumed and commercial sales value.

Pickling has retained its popularity —long after serving its purpose as a major means of food preservation— simply because we enjoy the provoking tastes that shock our palates. Pickles indeed taste good by themselves, but perhaps even more important are what they do for the flavors of other foods.

Their pungent aromas and sharp flavors combined with cool crispness sharpen our awareness of the flavors of other foods. Thus the term "condiment" or "compliment."

But what about Cleopatra and those who followed thinking pickles contributed to health? They were indeed correct. Recent research at Michigan State University has shown that the vitamin A content of fresh produce is actually *increased* through the pickling process.

Even though some of the vitamin C is decreased, pickles still retain richer deposits of the vitamin than other processed foods. The less processed pickle types retain a much greater amount of vitamin C. Vinegar prevents oxidation which allows the vitamin to escape from cut surfaces. This plus the fact that vinegar itself is good for you affirms that pickles make an important contribution to health.

20th Century pickling

A "pickle" is any fruit, vegetable, meat, or combination preserved primarily by the use of vinegar and/or salt. They may be honeyed, sugared, saccharined, peppered, dilled, spiced, diced, chopped, mixed, soured, fermented, stripped, chipped, sauced, brined, or wined. The possibilities are phenomenal.

VEGETABLE PICKLES may be cured by either *fermentation* (brining) for several weeks and then flavored as desired (dill, sweet, mustard). Or they may be *fresh-packed* by a quick-brining process, drained and mixed with vinegar and spices. (See pages 16-25 for details).

FRUIT PICKLES are usually simmered in a sweet-sour syrup with vinegar or lemon juices and spices.

PICKLED MEATS OR SEAFOOD may follow one of the methods for vegetable pickles or offer a slight departure. Vegetables, fruits, meats, or seafood may simply be *marinated* for short periods.

RELISHES are chopped or ground fruits and/or vegetables with vinegar and spices.

CHUTNEYS are prepared from chopped fruits and/or vegetables with nuts, spices and vinegars added before simmering.

CATSUPS and SAUCES may be made from fruits, vegetables, or combinations in many varieties.

VINEGAR-MAKING can be quite simple or become a connoisseur's hobby through experimenting with unlimited flavor combinations. See pages 76-79.

For many years "pickle" meant the traditional cucumber. Dilled beans or pickled okra pods were highly prized conversation items at parties. Today they are a part of many Americans' routine diets. Virtually any fruit or vegetable, as well as many meats, can be pickled.

Your very own pickles can be a highly personal thing; created to suit your own individual taste or needs, or the tastes of family and friends with whom you will be sharing your product. Alternative approaches to the use of sugar and/or artificial preservatives are as near as your pickle crock.

Since almost anything that can be eaten can be pickled, the only limitation is your imagination. In this book we offer you many ideas to start you on your way.

Some of our recipes beginning on page 28 are updated versions of family treasures that have been shared with us by fourth-generation cooks. Others are fresh, innocent ideas from young novice cooks who dared try something new.

Canning jar manufacturers have perfected the standard recipes for dills, sweets, mustards, chow chow.

Other pungent, piquant pickles are ideas from home economists with state university Cooperative Extension Services. The best cooks in Catahoula Parish, Louisiana, sent us their prize-winners. Our sampling of pickling cooks include a sea captain of Scandinavian origin, a professional cookbook writer, a couple who have lived on a secluded wilderness farm for 50 years and are passionate picklers, a New York composer who is a master of international cuisine, an Alaskan fisherman . . . .

When the pickler gardens

The old-time farm, fruit and vegetable garden fostered the full joy of pickling. Canning and other methods of preserving were the order of the day, but pickling was the creator's delight; the hallmark of the farm or ranch. There were surpluses to draw on. There was the annual shower of walnuts and almonds. What to do with all the figs? There was more cabbage than storage space. Turnips, onions, beets and green tomatoes were harvested at their perfect pickling size. There was room for citron, pickling cucumbers, gherkins and dill growing high. In season there were presents from neighboring orchards—lugs of peaches and plums and pears.

Today's apartment dwellers, non-gardeners and small space gardeners find ways to satisfy the farm-ranch preserving style. They know well the local harvest dates. The countryside is their supermarket. They locate the specialists—in Oriental and continental vegetables; in blackberries, strawberries, raspberries, blueberries, or whatever crop is adapted. Direct sales, grower to consumer, are increasing every year through U-Pick-It farms and orchards and roadside markets.

Up to a point, shopping the countryside for vegetables and fruit will satisfy the needs of the most enthusiastic pickler, but the pickler who gardens does enjoy a few special advantages.

When, with pickling on your mind, you plan a garden, read catalogs, buy seeds or transplants, you become a very special kind of gardener. Your interest in vegetable varieties takes on the pickler's concern. Are there pickling varieties?

One general answer that makes good sense is that a fresh vegetable of good eating quality will have good quality when preserved. A more specific answer would be that certain

varieties of cucumbers, onions and tomatoes are more useful to the pickler than other varieties.

Take tomatoes, for example. In a pickler's garden green tomatoes never go to waste. And green tomatoes are hard to come by in any market.

The small green tomato, which when pickled outshines the customary cocktail olive, is definitely a home garden item. The varieties 'Red Cherry,' 'Tiny Tim ' and 'Small Fry' are candidates for the cocktail pickle honor. All are heavy producers of cherry sized fruit in clusters. 'Red Cherry' is a rank grower. In a hanging basket it will drape down 3 to 4 feet. 'Tiny Tim' grows only 15 inches tall and is easily grown in 8-inch pots, window boxes or hanging baskets. 'Small Fry' bears 1-inch fruits by the hundreds—8 to 10 in a cluster—on a 30-inch vine. It's an ideal hanging basket plant.

Cucumber Varieties

If you are a long-time cucumber grower you know something about the recent developments in cucumber varieties and can read the seed catalogs with full understanding.

However, if you are choosing varieties for the first time there are words which need some explanation.

The catalogs do divide cucumbers into *slicing* varieties and *pickling* varieties. Or in *slicing, dual purpose* and *pickling* varieties. Some claim that "cucumbers may be harvested at almost any age. Different sizes may be picked at the same time; small ones for sweet pickles, larger ones for bread and butter pickles or dill pickles."

It is true that all cucumbers should be picked in the immature stage, but a *slicing* variety that is just right at 8 inches long does not have the pickling quality when they are small, sweet-pickle size.

In some areas you may be able to grow your choice of varieties without damage from the several cucumber diseases. But in most areas scab and mosaic are serious diseases, and if they don't put an end to your hopes for a bumper crop, downy and powdery mildew or anthracnose will. *The best insurance for success with cucumbers is to choose a disease resistant variety.*

Some examples of disease resistant slicing varieties are:

EARLY SURECROP. All-America Selection. (58 days from seed to maturity.) Strong vigorous vine with large leaves producing straight 8 to 9-inch fruit, 2½ inches in diameter. White Spine. Resistant to mosaic and downy mildew.

TRIUMPH. All-America Selection. (63 days.) Vine vigorous and compact. Produces a high percentage of No. 1 fruits (7½ to 8 inches) under adverse conditions. Fruits slow to become oversize. Resistant to mosaic and downy mildew.

VICTORY. All-America Selection. (60 days.) Produces under a wide range of conditions. Straight, smooth 8-inch fruit. White Spine. Tolerant to scab, mosaic and powdery mildew. Some tolerance to anthracnose.

There are many more disease resistant varieties. Some are hybrids, some are open pollinated, some are true dwarfs, some are white spined, some are black spined, some are gynoecious hybrids.

Whether a cucumber is white-spined or black-spined has nothing to do with its quality when pickled. The white spined variety may have more eye appeal as the spines disappear. Burpee's catalog explains this "spine" business: "Cucumbers are divided into families, 'White Spine' and 'Black Spine.' The spines are the miniature stickers that protrude from the warts when fruits are young. White spine cucumbers turn creamy white when old; black spine varieties turn yellowish orange." Most gardeners never leave cucumbers on the vines long enough to see which color they turn. But if you walk away from a "white spine" vine when the frost hits it and come back at Christmastime, the cucumbers will be white.

Another word that may slow you up in reading the description of a variety is "gynoecious." These are varieties with all female (almost) flowers. In the regular old cucumber the male blossoms greatly outnumber the female or fruiting blossoms; and in addition the male blossoms open first. Then, about a week later you see the female flowers with baby cucumbers at their bases.

There is no delayed setting of fruit with the all-female (gynoecious) hybrids. They set fruit with the first blossoms and thus set fruit closer to the base of the plant.

Another new development in cucumber breeding is the introduction of the dwarf or bush type. David W. Davis of the University of Minnesota writes: "Bush cucumber varieties have been under development for a long time. Some of those available trace their parentage to a very small dwarf parent type developed many years ago by A. E. Hutchins at the University of Minnesota. In cucumber, the bush and semi-bush types have seen more use by pickle manufacturing companies for mechanical harvesting.

Only recently have bush varieties been available to the gardener. 'Patio Pik' is perhaps the best known. Others advertised as having compact vines, such as 'Mincu' and 'Tiny Dill', actually are of normal vining character but the vines are somewhat less vigorous than other vining types."

In order to review the availability of cucumber varieties we checked the following catalogs very carefully:

Burgess Seed & Plant Co., Box 2000, Galesburg, MI 49053

W. Atlee Burpee Co., Philadelphia, PA, 19132; Clinton, IA 52732; Riverside, CA 92502.

Farmer Seed & Nursery Co., Faribault, MN 55021

Joseph Harris Co., Moreton Farm, Rochester, NY 14624

Henry Field Seed & Nursery Co., 407 Sycamore St., Shenandoah, IA 51601

Earl May Seed & Nursery Co., 6032 Elm St., Shenandoah, IA 51601

Stokes Seeds, Box 528, Main P.O., Buffalo, NY 14240; St. Catherine's, Ontario, Canada

Here's how they view the pickling varieties:

WISCONSIN SMR 18. 54 days. "One of the leading commercial pickles and fine for home gardens, too. It is early, productive and uniform, and the pickles are well shaped, firm and brine well. They are medium green in color, well warted and moderately ridged. Carries resistance to scab and mosaic." Harris Co. description; widely available.

OHIO MR. 57 days. "The new National Pickle type. Mosaic-resistant; vigorous, healthy vines produce a tremendous yield. Stay green and produce through the whole season. Five hills in our Test Garden produced 534 fruits and were still coming when frost hit. Two common kinds produced only 222 and 152. Has become canner's choice for fancy pickles." Earl May Co. description. Also available from Burpee Seed Co.

TINY DILL. 55 days. "Grows on compact 2-ft. vines. Needs little space, bears finger length cukes so desirable for whole dill pickles, long before others. Grow all you'll need in a few square feet even in northern gardens." Farmer Co. description.

WEST INDIA GHERKIN. 60 days. "Used extensively for very small pickles or relish. They have a splendid flavor. Vines produce an astonishingly large crop of small, burr-like fruits, 2 to 3 inches long and 1 to 1½ inches thick. The bright green skin is covered with fleshy prickles." W. Atlee Burpee Co. description.

PATIO PIK. 57 days. Dwarf cucumber developed especially for the patio and small garden. Plants have an upright habit, with short runners. Produces all female blooms. Every bloom sets a fruit. Just the right size for slicing, dills or fancy pickles." Earl May Co. description.

SALTY. 53 days. "One of the first white spine gynoecious hybrids with a high tolerance to scab as well as mosaic, powdery and downy mildew. Superior pickling characteristics and long lasting dark green colour, even in large sizes. Growers who are used to harvesting black spined pickles like 'Pioneer,' just before they turn light green, should be careful that the darker green fruit of 'Salty' do not become over mature before they realize it. 'Salty' has blunt shoulders and a uniform cylindrical shape. Excellent for "fresh pack" pickles or "salt stock".

LEMON CUCUMBER. 65 days. "A real cucumber that grows about the size and color of a large lemon. The flesh is white and has a remarkable sweet flavor, quite different from other cucumbers and very delicious. Highly esteemed both for slicing and pickling, they are ripe when first starting to turn yellow, but may be used either green or ripe." Harris Co. description.

Those little onions

Universally recommended for pickling is the 'White Portugal' or 'Silverskin.' When grown for pickling, seeds are sown 3 or 4 times as thick as usual. It is mild in flavor with snowy white, waxy skin. Harvest when cocktail size. The bulb will develop into a large, flat, fine-grained onion good for fall storage.

Japanese pickling melons

Seed of these pickling melons are available from mail order firms specializing in Oriental vegetables. One, 'Oshira Uri,' produces long oval shaped, light green fruits which turn white when mature. Medium thick crisp flesh. The variety 'Ao-Uri' bears dark green fruits 10 to 12 inches long, 4 to 4½ inches in diameter.

Beets and more

The Pickler's Garden might include Burpee's 'Golden Beet' just to see how well this unique variety pickles. Perhaps the pickler will have a favorite cabbage variety for kraut. Which watermelon makes the best pickles? Which variety of peppers? Which fresh herbs are essential? Answers to such questions must be left to the individual pickler.

Stocking the kitchen

Everything you need in equipment and ingredients for pickling—from crocks to vinegars.

There is very little specialized equipment needed for pickling. Anyone who's done any canning will have it all. But if you haven't canned, don't be distressed; the equipment is common, easily located and its usage for food preparation and the canning process is easy to comprehend.

Costs are minimal in home pickling. Especially in light of the money saved in putting up one's own food. Remember, too, that pickling ware, if looked after, is perpetually reusable.

While you'll need some specific ingredients, they are readily available and not costly. The average kitchen larder will have all but a slim percentage of the ingredients required for pickling.

Equipment

The quick fresh-pack method of pickling, in which vinegar is the main preservative, only requires some fairly deep containers. Large saucepans, even soup pots, will do. Enamelware, stainless steel, or glassware is best.

> It's imperative *not* to use iron, brass, copper, or zinc (galvanized), or unclean aluminum pots since they may chemically react with the acids and salts of the pickling mixture.

Pickling done with the long term brining and fermentation methods usually calls for larger quantities, thus larger receptacles. Stone crocks, kegs, or barrels are used. The ideal keg or barrel should be of hardwood, and either be enamel, glass, or paraffin lined. Any such container will require a lid, slightly smaller than the container's inside diameter, to keep the pickles submerged in brine. These containers must be watertight and should be scrupulously cleaned; any foreign residues or odors will certainly

affect the end product. (A lye solution, as per directions on the label, left standing for two days is sufficient to sweeten most any container. Be extremely cautious when using lye, following manufacturer's directions very carefully. You may need to re-paraffin the interior of a barrel after cleaning with lye.)

The proper utensils make pickling a lot easier; it's wise never to put your hands into the pickling mixture, as your body chemistry may affect the solution. Remember, too, that there will be a good deal of boiling involved. You will need a slotted spoon, some large forks, a pair of tongs, some sharp knives and probably a wooden spoon or two. Proper pans are equally important: stainless steel is best.

You also may require cleaning brushes for the preparation of food, a skimmer for removing scum from the mixture, a wide-mouthed funnel, a kitchen scale (especially for sauerkraut) and some cheesecloth or muslin for making spice bags. Particular techniques may call for more specialized equipment such as a food mill, kraut cutter, or thermometer.

An essential piece of equipment is some type of large kettle for heat processing. There are commercial water-bath canners available but a large deep pot will easily suffice. The pot must have a rack in the bottom so that water may circulate beneath the jar. It should also be deep enough to allow an inch of water above the top of the jar and to account for boil-over. Naturally the larger the pot the more jars that can be heat processed at one time. Lifting the hot canning jars from the boiling water is a ticklish business. The tool made for just that purpose is worth the investment.

The other way to heat process is with a steam-canner. It achieves a high heat (240 degrees to the water bath's 212 degrees) and not only cuts heat processing time but is more desirable for preserving certain types of low-acid foods. Needless to say, both the water bath and the steam canner need a heat source sufficient to keep them at a vigorous boil for extended periods of time.

The vast majority of pickled products end up stored in glass jars. Canning jars go by many names: Mason, Ball, Bernardin, Kerr (common brand names). These jars are easily identifiable by their special capping systems. They have a rubber seal, either separate or attached to a flat circular top and a screw cap either whole or centerless depending on the type of rubber seal.

It's important that these jars, caps and seals be unchipped, uncracked, or unblemished. Any imperfection in the sealing capability of the jar, which could admit air, will ruin the contents. Any damaged pieces should be replaced. Use new lids or rubber seals each time.

Do not put up pickled products in commercial jars such as mayonnaise, pickle, or peanut butter jars. They do not seal properly, are not made to withstand heat processing, or may explode during pickling process.

Don't forget labels. Some cooks note the recipe source on the label so they'll know whether the recipe is worth repeating. You don't want to be eating your latest cannings first, so date everything. Non-glass containers must be labelled; there's no fun in opening two crocks of the same thing.

Pickling in large quantities may be desirable for economic reasons. If so, a keg or barrel might serve you well. Be sure, however, to find the right kind. As with all canning, the poorly made or imperfect container can only result in spoiled food and wasted time. The costs of home pickling are minimal enough without trying to cut any corners on the few items that can't be compromised. The charts on pages 10 and 11 illustrate virtually all the equipment you will need for home pickling.

Pickling equipment suppliers

Order catalogues to find crocks, canners, kettles and other equipment.

✔BAZAAR DE LA CUISINE, INTERNATIONAL, 1003 Second Ave., New York, NY 10022

✔COLONIAL GARDEN KITCHENS, 270 Merrick Rd., Valley Stream, NY 11582.

✔HERTERS, INCORPORATED, ($1.) Department 51, Waseca, MN 56093.

✔J. C. PENNEY COMPANY, INCORPORATED, 1301 Avenue of the Americas, New York, NY 10019.

✔MAID OF SCANDINAVIA COMPANY, ($1.) 3244 Raleigh Avenue, Minneapolis, MN 55416.

✔MONTGOMERY WARD AND COMPANY, 419 West Chicago Avenue, Chicago, IL 60607.

✔MOTHER'S GENERAL STORE, Box 506, Flat Rock, NC 28731

✔NASCO, 901 Janesville, Ft. Atkinson, WI 53538; or 1524 Princeton Avenue, Modesto, CA 95382.

✔PAPRIKAS WEISS, ($1.) 1546 Second Avenue, New York, NY 10026.

✔R. AND R. MILLS COMPANY, INC., 45 West First North, Smithfield UT 84335.

✔SEARS ROEBUCK AND COMPANY, 2650 East Olympic Boulevard, Los Angeles, CA 90051; or 4640 Roosevelt Boulevard, Philadelphia, PA 19132, or apply for a catalogue through your local retail outlet.

✓SMITHFIELD IMPLEMENT COMPANY, 99 North Main Street, Smithfield UT 84321.
✓VERMONT COUNTRY STORE, Weston, VT 05161.

Ingredients

There are two basic food elements in the pickling process. The fruit-vegetable-meat to be pickled and the pickling mixture called brine, syrup or marinade.

We cannot over-emphasize the importance of selecting top quality, garden-fresh produce for pickling. It is not worth your time or effort to use less than the best available ingredients.

The pickling mixture

VINEGAR. Common distilled white vinegar is best for pickling. It should be sediment-free and four to six per cent acetic acid, sometimes labeled as 40 to 60 grain strength. Most commercial vinegars are a standard five per cent acetic acid. Use undiluted unless the recipe specifies otherwise.

Distilled white vinegar does not impart any coloring in the pickling process. A cider, malt, or wine vinegar can be used if it is of the correct acidity, though these vinegars will contribute their own color and flavor to the pickles. If you like the flavors of these vinegars by all means use them. But distilled white vinegar will be suggested in most recipes. In any case, avoid long boiling of vinegar, to prevent loss of acetic acid.

> The use of homemade vinegars in pickling recipes can be risky and is not recommended because their quality and degree of acidity is difficult to determine.

Edible lactic acid is available from your druggist and may be used, partially or completely, as a substitute for vinegar. Remember to use only one-tenth the amount of lactic acid as of vinegar. Edible lactic acid is preferred by those who like a less sharp flavoring than vinegar for their pickles.

SUGAR. White granulated beet or cane sugar is used in pickling. Brown sugar may be called for in a few specific recipes. The use of brown sugar will significantly darken the pickle.

Honey may be used in place of white sugar. Light honeys, such as alfalfa or clover, are superior to the darker, stronger honeys that tend to discolor and overpower other ingredients. In recipes that call for boiling, it may be necessary to boil a little longer with honey to thicken the syrup because of the natural water content of the honey. Add honey to taste, most cooks use equal amounts; although many agree that it takes less honey than sugar for the same degree of sweetness.

Pickling can be done with sugar substitutes. But there are differences between products such as Sucaryl and Saccharin and they should be used according to their manufacturer's directions. For more information about sugarless pickling write to the manufacturer of the substitute or: American Diabetics Association, Inc. 18 East 48th, New York, NY 10017.

SALT. Both a preservative and a flavoring. There is a salt specifically marketed as "pickling salt." It's preferred of course, but failing to find it, pure granulated salt is next best and completely satisfactory. Table salts, both iodized and plain are undesirable as they contain additives that can cloud the brine and discolor the pickles.

Some pickling guides will tell you that coarse salt, dairy salt, kosher, rock, or sack salt, as well as sea salt are acceptable. In our mind they all have drawbacks.

Kosher salt, for example, is a good but weak relative to the others; coarse salt dissolves too slowly and tends to lump, which prevents even distribution in the pickling mixture. Pickling salt is even-flowing and of certain strength: by far the easiest and most successful to work with.

WATER. Soft water is desirable for pickling. The dissolved minerals in hard water can only interfere with the pickling process. If only hard water is available it should be boiled, its surface scum skimmed away, and the water left to sit for 24 hours. Water should then be drawn off the top of the receptacle without disturbing any sediment.

An easier alternative than boiling, if you live in a hard water area, is to buy distilled water. Try pickling both ways and decide for yourself whether the cost is justified.

SPICES AND HERBS. Pickles readily adopt the flavors of seasonings which add immeasurably to the tastiness of your finished foodstuffs. Spices and herbs are always best for pickling when they're fresh.

Spices and herbs can be added loose to mixtures that are later strained, or, more efficiently, combined in a tied spice-bag of cheesecloth or muslin. The spice-bag is then used in the cooking mixtures or cold vinegars just like a teabag.

In those recipes calling for freshly ground spices employ a peppermill. For nuts and seeds use a mortar and pestle or crush in a saucer with the backside of a spoon.

While whole fresh spices and herbs are superior, dry and powdered forms are usable. They may, however, cloud the pickling mixture. One should use only about one-fourth as much of a dry spice or herb as fresh, and about one-eighth as much of powdered. Measure carefully the first time you make a recipe for fear of ending up with a single dominating flavor in your pickling mixture. Next time you'll know what to add or subtract to suit your tastebuds. See seasoning chart on pages 94-95.

ALUM, LIME AND COLORING. If pickling is done properly there is no need for crispening or coloring additives. The use of alum and/or lime is superfluous and used in excess can cause digestive upset. Coloring agents, which alter natural vegetable color, are not recommended. Never use copper sulfate or vitrial as called for in some older pickle recipes.

LYE. This necessary ingredient in the time-consuming procedure of pickling olives is caustic; use it with extreme care.

Ingredients chart

	Preferred	Conditionally Acceptable	Unacceptable
Vinegar	Distilled White	Cider, Malt, Wine Edible lactic acid	Homemade
Sugar	White granulated, cane or beet Honey, light	Brown Honey, dark Sugar substitutes	Powdered
Salt	Pickling	Pure granulated, coarse, dairy, kosher, rock, sack, sea	Table, iodized and uniodized Flavored
Water	Soft Bottled distilled	Hard, boiled and skimmed	Hard
Spices, Herbs	Fresh	Dried Powdered	Herb and Spice salts

A pickler's equipment guide

This chart illustrates virtually all the equipment one might need for home pickling. Remember that implements made of copper, brass, iron, zinc (galvanized) and unclean aluminum are not to be used for pickling. Stainless steel, enamel and glassware are best.

Item		Amount	Material and Size
Long handled spoons and forks		2	Stainless steel, wood, or plastic with handles long enough to keep hands a safe distance from heat sources.
Slotted spoons		2	Stainless steel, wood, or plastic with long handles.
Ladle		1	Long handled soup ladles of plastic, wood, or stainless steel.
Scum skimmer		1	Wooden, stainless steel, or combination of wood and wire with long handles.
Measuring spoons		1 set	Plastic, glass, or stainless steel from ¼ teaspoon to tablespoon.
Paring knife		1	About six inches, preferably wooden handle and steel blades, very sharp.
French knife		1	Either blunt end or tapered steel blade with wooden handle; about 12 inches long overall.
Butcher knife		1	12 to 14 inches, wooden handle with steel blade.
Colander		1	Enamel, stainless steel, or plastic large enough to hold at least two quarts of produce. Legs for drainage are preferred.
Food brushes		2	4-8 inches with plastic or wooden handles and stiff bristles.
Food chopper or grinder (fine, medium, coarse blades)		1	Stainless steel; usually have screw on device for clamping to cabinet in stationary position.
Food mill		1	Stainless steel or plastic, large enough to hold at least one quart of produce.
Food scale		1	Metal with stainless or plastic tray for produce. Scale for weighing up to 25 pounds at once.
Fruit press		1	Wood, stainless steel, or plastic, holding up to two quarts.
Grater		1	Plastic or stainless steel with various size cutting blades.
Jar lifter or tongs		1	Stainless steel with plastic, wood, or rubberized handle or grip.

Item		Amount	Material and Size
Kitchen scissors		1 pair	Stainless steel or plastic with blades at least 6 inches long.
Measuring cups		1 set	Glass, stainless steel, or plastic from ¼ cup to quart.
Sieve		1	Nylon or non-tarnish metal, holds up to one quart at a time.
Timer		1	Metal or plastic to measure up to 1 hour. Darkroom timers can measure seconds.
Vegetable peeler		1	Stainless with rotary blade.
Wide-mouthed funnel		1	Plastic, metal, or glass to hold at least 1 cup at a time.
Wire basket		1	Stainless steel to fit inside canning kettle below.
Large kettle or deep metal pail or metal can or water-bath canner or steam pressure canner		1	At least 12 inches deep; stainless steel or enameled is preferable. Should have fitted cover.
Saucepans		2-3	Enamel, stainless steel, glass, porcelain, or newly-cleansed aluminum holding from 3-5 quarts.
Glass jars (also lids and rubber seals)			Glass with metal lids, seals and rings in sizes from ½ pint to 1 quart. Make sure glass is heat tempered to resist breakage during processing.
Crocks or large jars		1-3	Ceramic, stone, or glass from 1 gallon up.
Kegs or barrels		1-2	Stone, crockery, enamel-glass-paraffin-lined kegs and barrels best (with five-inch bungs, inside lid).
Cheesecloth, muslin, or tea bag			Wrapped cheesecloth packages are available in supermarkets. Stainless teabags can be used.
Labels			Plain or fancy gummed, large enough to contain all information desired.
Calendar		1	Monthly, with space for writing pickling schedule.

Best market buys on fresh produce

Vast new world-wide growing areas, jet-age shipping, improved refrigeration and storage and greenhouse growing combine to make most vegetables and fruits available to the home pickler throughout the year. This chart is a guide to the seasonal peaks at which time you can get the best quality and quantity for the least money. Only a few items remain more or less stable all year.

Produce	Jan.	Feb.	Mar.	April	May	June	July	Aug.	Sept.	Oct.	Nov.	Dec.
Apples									■	■	■	■
Apricots					■	■	■					
Artichokes				■	■					■		
Asparagus			■	■	■	■						
Bananas	■	■	■	■	■	■	■	■	■	■	■	■
Beans						■	■	■				
Beets						■	■	■				
Blackberries						■	■	■				
Blueberries						■	■	■				
Broccoli	■	■	■							■	■	■
Brussels Sprouts	■	■								■	■	■
Cabbage	■	■	■	■	■	■	■	■	■	■	■	■
Carrots	■	■	■	■	■	■	■	■	■	■	■	■
Cauliflower									■	■	■	
Celery	■	■	■	■	■	■	■	■	■	■	■	■
Corn					■	■	■	■	■			
Cucumbers					■	■	■	■				
Cranberries									■	■	■	
Coconuts										■	■	■
Cherries						■	■					
Dates										■	■	■
Eggplant								■	■			
Figs						■	■	■	■			
Garlic			■	■								
Grapes								■	■	■		
Grapefruit	■	■	■	■	■							
Horseradish			■	■								
Jerusalem artichoke	■	■										
Kiwis	■	■									■	■
Kumquats	■	■	■									■
Lemons	■	■	■	■	■	■	■	■	■	■	■	■
Limes	■	■	■	■	■	■	■	■	■	■	■	■
Mangoes					■	■	■	■				
Mushrooms	■	■	■	■	■	■	■	■	■	■	■	■
Muskmelons						■	■	■	■			
Nectarines							■	■	■			
Okra						■	■	■	■			
Onions	■	■	■	■	■	■	■	■	■	■	■	■
Oranges	■	■	■	■	■							
Papayas					■	■						
Parsnips	■	■										
Peaches						■	■	■	■			
Pears								■	■	■	■	
Peppers								■	■			
Persimmons										■	■	■
Pineapple			■	■	■	■						
Plums						■	■	■	■			
Pomegranates										■	■	
Radish			■	■	■							
Raspberries						■	■					
Rhubarb				■	■	■						
Rutabagas								■	■			
Spinach			■	■	■							
Strawberries				■	■	■						
Tangerines	■										■	■
Tomatoes					■	■	■					
Turnips										■	■	■

Artichokes' outer lower leaves should be removed and discarded. Slice off the thorny tip with a sharp knife and cut thorns from remaining leaf tips with kitchen scissors. Or remove all leaves to discover the heart.

Attractive julienne cuts are made by cutting off a thin slice from the rounded side of peeled carrots so the vegetable will lie flat, then slicing ⅛ inch thick. Lay slices flat and cut into pieces like match-sticks.

Cut diagonal slices of stalky vegetables by using a French knife blade as a pivot, slicing through the stalk at an angle. The other hand is used to feed the stalk after a cut has been made.

Preparation of fruits and vegetables

Individual recipes will often stipulate the specialized preparations of food. This chart indicates the techniques used for the most common pickles. All food must be washed thoroughly and rinsed several times. If scrubbing is necessary to remove dirt, do so. Any imperfect or overripe foods must not be used. You will need a paring knife. A French knife is also useful as is a steamer, a colander and a shredder.

Fruits

Apples	Core and peel. Slice apples into halves or quarters. To prevent darkening, dip raw apples in a gallon of water containing 2 tablespoons of salt and 2 tablespoons of vinegar.
Apricots	Immerse in boiling water for thirty seconds or so to loosen skins. Plunge in cold water to cool, then peel. Leave whole or cut in half, removing seeds.
Blackberries Blueberries Gooseberries Loganberries Raspberries (red or black)	Wash a quart at a time, inspecting closely. Snap off caps and stems.
Cherries	Stem and remove pits, using a cherry pitter for best results. Unpitted cherries should be pricked with a needle to prevent bursting.
Cranberries	Use only very firm berries. Stem.
Figs	Discard overly ripe figs. Do not stem.
Grapes	Eliminate all soft grapes. Gently stem.
Grapefruit	Peel as you would an apple, cutting deep enough to remove all the white membrane. Pull grapefruit into halves. Run a thin knife between pulp and skin, keeping each section intact. Discard seeds.
Guavas	Peel, removing blossom and stem end. Cut into halves, scrape out pulp.
Loquats	Remove blossom ends and stem. Cut in half and remove seeds.
Mangoes	Peel. Cut horizontal slices away from hard seed in center.
Melons	Slice off ends, then cut in halves. Cut into one inch thick slices. Peel and cut into smaller wedges.
Nectarines	Immerse in boiling water for thirty seconds or so to loosen skins. Plunge in cold water to cool, peel. Leave whole or cut in half, removing seeds.
Papayas	Peel and cut in half. Scrape out black seed and discard. Cut as desired.
Peaches	Boil thirty seconds or so to loosen skins. Dip in cold water to cool and immediately skin. Cut in half, remove seeds. Scrape cavities to remove pink or red fibers.
Pears	Peel, being careful not to remove too much fruit and to retain the shape of the pear. Cut into halves or quarters and core. Treat as apples to prevent darkening.
Pineapple	Cut off ends. Slice horizontally into flat rounds. Peel and remove core from each ring. Cut into wedges.
Plums	Remove stems. Prick skins with needle to prevent bursting.
Strawberries	Choose firm, completely red, berries. Remove all sand in washing and remove caps.

Vegetables

Artichokes	Remove hard tip and drier outer leaves. Trim base flat so artichoke will stand upright. Snip off tips of remaining leaves.
Asparagus	Remove paper-like scales from sides of stalks, as well as tough woody ends. Leave asparagus whole, cut to fit jar, or cut into one inch lengths.
Beans (green, snap, wax)	Snap or cut both ends off bean. Leave whole or cut into two inch pieces.
Beans (lima, butter)	Snip outer edges with scissors. Remove beans from shells.
Beets	Leave two inches of stem and tap root. Boil beets until skins can be slipped off, removing stem and root. Leave whole or slice.
Broccoli	Trim ends of stems. Leave stalks whole, slicing lengthwise. Cut into two inch pieces.
Brussels Sprouts	Trim base. Remove any blemished leaves. Use whole.
Cabbage	Discard blemished leaves. Cut into halves and shred with knife or shredder.
Carrots	Scrub and scrape with vegetable peeler. Slice, dice, or leave whole.
Cauliflower	Remove outside leaves. Trim stem. Slice lengthwise then cut into smaller pieces, leaving flowerets whole.
Celery	Separate individual stalks. Trim leaves and ends. Cut into two inch pieces or longer.
Corn	Remove husks and silk with vegetable brush. Use on cob or slice kernels from cob with sharp knife, leaving kernel bases on cob. Discard any pieces of cob.
Cucumber	Peel only if skin is extra tough or waxy. Use whole or slice into chips or long strips.
Greens (turnip, kale, mustard, beet tops, chard)	Remove tough stems and cores. Follow specific recipe.
Mushrooms	Scrub thoroughly. Trim ends. Leave whole, halve, or quarter.
Onions	Remove paper-like outer skins or loose skin of green onions. Trim roots and tops. Halve or slice.
Parsnips	Scrub, pare with a vegetable scraper and rewash. Use whole or sliced.
Peppers (green)	Cut in half. Remove stems and seeds. Cut into strips.
Pimento	Boil or roast pimentos until skins can be rubbed off. Remove skins, ends, and seeds. Flatten peppers.
Radishes	Scrub. Cut off root end. Use whole or sliced.
Squash (zucchini, chayote)	Scrub. Cut ends but do not peel. Use whole or sliced.
Rhubarb	Use tender young stalks. Trim leaves and ends. Cut into one inch lengths.
Tomatoes	Scald tomatoes briefly to loosen skins. Skin. Use whole or cut into halves or quarters. Cut out stem end.

The pickling process

The how-to of pickling—fermentation as well as time-saving fresh-pack methods. Processing for longer keeping. Avoiding problems before you start.

Colorful, zesty chow-chow relish not only adds great flavor to hamburgers, but is excellent with many other dishes and is simple and fun to make.

For the purist the long term brining process or fermentation is at the center of the art of pickling. This time-honored method utilizes a controlled fermentation process. Sauerkraut is a most renowned product of this method. It is fermentation that gives pickles the snappy, sharp taste that vinegar can almost, but not quite, duplicate. It is a process that can take months and must be closely observed.

Long term brining also can be done without allowing fermentation to occur. High salt quantities and vinegar are enlisted to subjugate the fermentation causing bacteria. Such pickles, made in heavy brine but not fermented, need to be bathed in water or water-vinegar solutions to remove some of their saltiness. This is done after brining is completed but before eating.

These long term processes are age-old and completely natural. You'll find the results well worth the longer effort and the standard by which the other pickling methods must be measured.

But most pickling is done employing a relatively short process. Fruits and relishes are quick pickled out of necessity. Vegetables can be quick pickled for convenience's sake. Recipes will vary greatly, of course, but the bare bones of good pickling involve three steps: the making of a pickling mixture, the containerizing of prepared food in that mixture and the heat processing of the jar and its contents before it is put away for storage.

Cucumbers, dill and garlic team up in varying methods to create an American classic—the dill pickle.

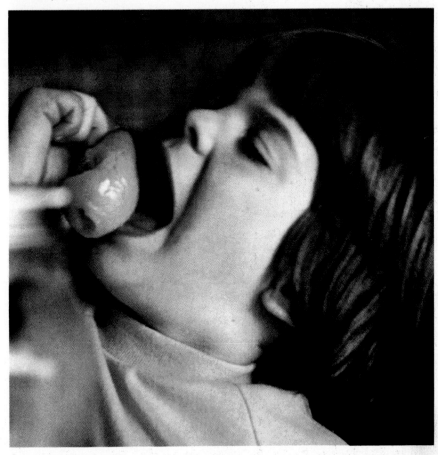

Some people can't even wait for a freshly pickled pear to get into the jar for storage. Pickling can be a creative project for the whole family.

15

The making of a pickle

Vegetables, after an overnight brining, are usually placed in a vinegar-based pickling liquid. It is the vinegar that will imbue them with that tangy, pickled taste. The vinegars will be differentiated on the basis of the herbs and spices added to them according to your preferences. The foods are then heat processed and stored.

Fruits, in general, are pickled in a slightly different manner than vegetables. They are immersed in a vinegar-sugar-based mixture, usually termed syrup. The sugar will account for the trademark of pickled fruits, the sweet-sour taste.

Relishes are also made with a vinegar-sugar-based mixture. The latter ingredient will be varied, in a chutney, for example, to achieve the degree of sweetness or sourness you desire. Relishes, as do all pickle products, lend themselves easily to delicate flavorings.

Pickle protection

Heat processing is the final step of the pickling procedure. Here many cooks and pickling authorities themselves come into disagreement. Many argue that the percentage of vinegar or the result of fermentation are sufficient to destroy any possibility of danger from botulism or other harmful microorganisms.

Even though this may come as quite a shock to seasoned picklers, our research found that most jar manufacturers and contemporary home economists are in agreement with the United States Department of Agriculture that all pickled products should be heat processed. We support this safety measure.

Heat processing does not alter the flavor of the pickled recipe. It merely heats the food and container to a level where all bacteria are killed, thus preventing spoilage.

Additionally, heat processing is the step that provides your jars with an airtight seal. This is absolutely essential to the safe storage of canned foods. Any food preserving method has its hazards. Pickling does too. But they can be minimized by following directions carefully, especially concerning packing and heat processing. Having followed all directions carefully, you'll have no cause for anxiety.

To sum up: pickling can be a short or long term process. In quick pickling vinegar replaces the lactic acid of the fermentation process in preserving the food. Quick pickled products might not have quite the taste and crispness of brined pickles but they're very close. Long term pickling, on the other hand, is done over weeks and months. The rewards of this method are in the unique tastes and textures of foods that have undergone the fermentation process. Most all kinds of food can be pickled. Done intelligently it's one of the safest ways of preserving foods.

For illustrated step-by-step procedures of the three basic pickling methods, see pages 18-23.

Never eat any pickles that are slimy, bad smelling, or that are frothy or soft. Do not even taste them. Dispose of them immediately. The accompanying chart can help eliminate these problems.

Make Kosher dills by the process described on pages 22 and 23. Your results will be a taste sensation and a rich source of vitamins.

A checklist of pickling problems

Problems	Causes	Prevention
Soft, slippery slimy pickles (discard pickles, spoilage is occurring)	a. Hard water b. Acid level too low c. Cooked too long or at too high a temperature d. Water bath too short, bacteria not destroyed e. Jars not airtight f. Jars in too warm a resting place	a. Boil water. See directions (Ingredients). b. Check acid level of vinegar; it must be 4-6%. Using homemade vinegar is not advised. c. Using a steam canner? Too-high heats are one of their minuses. d. Follow bath directions meticulously. e. Check seals and rims before using. f. Cans should be stored in a cooler spot.
Shriveled, tough pickles	a. Pickles overcooked b. Syrup too heavy c. Too strong a brine or vinegar solution d. Pickles not fresh enough at outset e. Fruit cooked too harshly in vinegar/sugar mixture	a. Recheck processing times and follow exactly. b. Combine salt, sugar and vinegar more evenly and slowly. c. Check recipe. Weaken brine or vinegar solution. d. Double-check with your source as to freshness. e. Cook more slowly at a slightly lower heat.
Dark, discolored pickles	a. Iron utensils used b. Copper, brass, iron, or zinc cookware used c. Hard water d. Metal lid corrosion e. Too great a quantity of powdered and dried spices used f. Iodized salt used	a. Using steel or wooden spoons is recommended. b. Enamel, glass, or stainless steel cookware is best. c. Boil water. See directions (Ingredients). d. Replace with new lids. e. Use fresh spices and herbs or cut back on the use of powdered and dried. f. Use pickling salt with no additives.
Murky liquid	a. Powdered and dried spices and herbs used	a. Try fresh herbs and spices or reduce amounts of dried and powdered.
Sediment	a. If pickles are firm, sediment is not unnatural. Could be harmless yeast growth or impurities in salt.	a. Use pure pickling salt
Hollow cucumbers	a. Poorly grown b. Not pickled when fresh c. Wrong variety	a. Hollow cucumbers usually float. Use them for relishes.

Sauerkraut—White scum present
    Slimy
    Dark color
	a. Air reaching kraut. Jar not sealed tightly.
	b. Not enough salt present during fermentation.
	c. Uneven salting during the brining process. Heat processed too long. Too much air contact during fermentation and jarring.
		a. Check seals.
		
		b. Be scrupulous about measurements in all recipes.
		c. Add salt only to the top of the brine; do not let it all slip to the bottom. Check heat processing times. Be sure that brine always covers the cabbage during fermentation and storage.

Cauliflower—Pinkish coloration	a. This isn't spoilage but a natural chemical change.	a. No cause for concern
Green Vegetables—Turn brown in jars	a. Overcooking or vegetables overripe to begin with.	a. Obey processing time limits. Find vegetables just slightly underripe.

Jars—Liquids boil out during water bath
    Lids will not hold seal
    Lids bulge
	a. Food packed too solidly in jars. If seal is made, however, there is no need to reprocess.
	b. Food between lid and rim of jar. Jar rim cracked or chipped. Rubber rims disintegrating or wearing out.
	c. Caps screwed too tightly during heat processing.
		a. Drive knife blade between jar sides and food to release trapped air.
		
		b. Wipe rims and lids carefully before sealing jars.
		
		c. Replace imperfect jars and lids. Tighten lids firmly, then release one-quarter turn before heat processing.

Fresh-pack pickling

There are unique and hard-earned tastes associated with lengthy brining explained on page 20-23 that can't be matched by any other pickling methods. But for many people the process is just too time and space consuming.

Enter the popular fresh-pack or quick-pickling method. So-called quick-pickling is achieved with techniques that, at most, require overnight brining.

Most of today's pickle recipes use this method and many are designed for quantities as small as that of a single jar. In this regard quick-pickling has many advantages over long-term brining or fermentation.

Many cooks who have never attempted pickling are amazed at the speed and simplicity of making delicious pickles by the fresh-pack method. In only an hour, or so, you can complete the entire job and enjoy the benefits for weeks or months to come.

The three general classes of fresh-pack pickling products are those of vegetables, fruits and relishes. All can be put up by the quick method; each requires a slightly different preparation and treatment.

Vegetables for quick-pickling will be in smaller pieces. Cucumbers, for example, should be little or else sliced. Standard procedure calls for up to overnight marination in some kind of salt solution or, perhaps, in salt alone. That's the extent of the brining process; the vegetables will then be drained and packed into jars and covered with hot liquid, or boiled in the pickling liquid. Vinegar, not lactic acid as in the fermented pickle, will act as the preservative.

Some recipes call for placing the fresh vegetables directly in the jar, adding seasonings and pouring liquids to cover before processing. The pickling process takes place in the jar.

1. Marinate fresh fruit or vegetable in a brine solution for the time period designated.

NOTE: These are the basic steps in Fresh-Pack pickling. Recipes for specific fruits and vegetables may modify some of them—and, of course, you will have to consult a recipe for the exact ingredients, amounts, and times for each individual product you wish to pickle.

2. Drain produce and put it in clean, sterilized mason jars, along with any large spice pieces (dill heads, etc.) called for in recipe. Leave 1" space at the top.

3. In a large pot, mix water, salt, vinegar, sugar and other spices (either loose or in a cheesecloth bag) as required. Bring to a boil (and, in some cases, simmer for the period) as called for in the recipe.

Fruits are usually not subjected to a brining process. They are either placed in the jar and covered with hot liquid, or they are steeped in a vinegar-spice-sugar syrup; simmered in this concoction for a definite period and then transferred, with the same syrup, into hot jars. There are variations on this theme according to the particular fruit and recipe. Fruit pickles are then sealed immediately and given a boiling-water bath.

Relishes may be simmered in a syrup or marinated for a short period before being placed in the jar and covered with the same liquid.

Marination is a form of quick pickling that may involve fruits, vegetables, meats, or various combinations.

This process calls for simply soaking the produce in a solution of vinegar and a blend of seasonings for a specified time—from a couple of hours to several days. Some will need occasional stirring or turning to cause equal penetration of the marinate throughout the fruit, vegetable, or meat.

Most marinated products should be kept under refrigeration throughout the entire process.

All fresh-pack pickled products are preserved with vinegar in some degree. Much of the fun in this kind

of pickling is in creating your own unique vinegar flavors by playing with the spice and herb content. As previously pointed out, using homemade vinegar is taboo, but you have carte blanche when it comes to flavoring any of the distilled white vinegars that are best for quick-pickling. See pages 76-79.

Quick-pickling, "quickies," or fresh-packing, done correctly, is the most thorough procedure for protecting your food from spoilage. The speed at which you work offers less exposure of the product to air than in longer methods of pickling. Some are kept under refrigeration, others can be processed as on pages 24-25.

4. Pour the hot pickling liquid into the jars. Be sure to cover the produce, but leave at least ¼″ (or head space designated in recipe) above the liquid.

5. Seal the jars and give them a boiling-water bath as described on pages 24 and 25.

Non-fermentation brining

Brining without fermentation is a process that will preserve vegetables for later use in pickling (although such vegetables can also be cooked in more orthodox ways after they've been desalted). Brining will give vegetables that unique "cured" taste and is worth the long wait and effort. You should remember that in a non-fermentation procedure you're only half-way to the finished pickle when brining is completed; the vegetables still have to be desalted and then jarred in a vinegar pickling mixture.

Salt-Vinegar Brining

The best candidates for the salt-vinegar brining method are the standby cucumbers, onions, and peppers but also many of the low-acid vegetables which, from a health standpoint, would be dangerous to subject to a fermentation process. This group includes carrots, cauliflower, celery, corn, peas, and snap beans.

The brine used is usually made according to this formula: four and one-half cups of salt (about three pounds) and one pint of vinegar for each gallon of water.

Vegetables must be weighed. In whatever size container you're using, maintain the ratio of one pint of brine to each pound of vegetables. If you're using glass jars, be sure that the brine completely covers the vegetables, then seal tightly. A crock or keg or barrel must have a weighted inside cover that will keep the vegetables submerged. These larger containers must then be sealed with paraffin. (Note: see end of section for desalting and further pickling procedures with brined vegetables.)

High-Salt Brining

This method of brining should be done in large containers: crocks, kegs, or barrels. The following general directions are designed for ten pound increments of vegetables. So be sure to weigh them carefully.

High-salt brining is best with carrots, cauliflower, cucumbers, green tomatoes, onions, peppers and snap beans.

The brine in this method consists of one pound of salt to each gallon of water. For cauliflower, onions and peppers use one and a half pounds of salt per gallon of water.

Pack the vegetables into the crocks or barrels. Remember that it will be easier if you use five or ten pound portions. Fill the containers with brine being sure that all the vegetables are completely submerged. Wrap the inside lid of the container with cheesecloth. A water-filled plastic bag provides a good weight on the inside lid. A day later add one pound of salt for each ten pounds of vegetables. Place this salt on top of the inside lid but underwater. Otherwise the salt will sink and be too strongly concentrated at the bottom. After one week remove the lid, skim off any scum, clean the sides of any ringed scum, wash the lid and wrap it anew in cheesecloth. Then replace the lid and add one-quarter of a pound of salt for each ten pounds of vegetables; again, place this in the water above the lid. Add this same amount at the ends of the second, third, fourth, fifth, and sixth weeks, as well as removing any scum that forms. The vegetables should be ready in six to eight weeks.

Freshening (Desalting)

Vegetables that have been brined will have to be freshened; they're simply too salty to eat after the brining treatment and, of course, you may now wish to make them into either sweet or sour pickles. The desalting procedure is simply one of bathing the vegetables in liquid to draw out some of the salt.

One method advocates soaking the vegetables in equal parts of vinegar and water. Another technique requires simmering in fresh water. For the latter, place the vegetables in a large pan of water and heat to simmering. Being careful not to boil, hold the simmer for twenty minutes. Then drain, add fresh water and heat to simmering again. Remove the pan from the heat. Let the vegetables stand in this water for twelve to fourteen hours. If the vegetables are still too salty soak them in cold water for another twelve hours.

The vegetables should be ready now for jarring in a vinegar mixture, according to specific recipes, for the final pickling.

1. Clean and weigh vegetables carefully. The weight determines the amount of brining liquid needed.

4. Place loose fitting lid (wooden disc or dinner plate) wrapped in cheesecloth over the vegetables along with something heavy to keep it submerged. A water-filled jar or plastic bag makes an excellent weight.

Note: These are the basic steps in Non-Fermentation Brining methods. Read the adjoining text for when these methods are appropriate, what vegetables they are used for and several recipe variations.

2. Mix brine according to the formula in the text.

3. Put vegetables in a large crock or barrel and cover them with the brine.

5. At intervals recommended in the text skim the scum from the brine and wipe any ring of scum from the sides. Also wash, rewrap and replace the submerged lid and weight . . .

6. . . . and add salt to the water *above* the lid.

7. At the end of the brining period affix a tight fitting lid to keep air out until vegetables are to be used. Paraffin may be used instead of a lid (see page 23) or you may seal the vegetables in jars with a boiling-water bath (see pages *24* and *25*).

Fermentation pickling

Certain vegetables can be pickled using a controlled fermentation process. This method produces a distinctly flavored vegetable. Who can forget sauerkraut?

In the fermentation process bacteria generate lactic acid from the vegetable sugars. For this reason some foods with low sugar contents such as asparagus, corn, peas, snap beans and spinach are unsuitable for fermented pickling. The whole point of one's technique in fermentation pickling is to promote a condition congenial to the creation of lactic acid, while suppressing any other organisms that might spoil the vegetables.

It is a long process that requires careful attention, perhaps more than any of the other pickling methods. The higher salt concentration and vinegar that would ordinarily deter fermentation and provide flavor are lessened in fermentation pickling to allow the sharp tasting lactic acid to form.

As in all long term brining processes it is important to have a closely regulated saline level in the brine. For fermentation pickling an eight per cent solution is best. That's about three-quarters of a pound of salt to each gallon of water. This level will maintain the salt's preservative qualities without destroying the lactic acid bacteria. The fermentation process is at its most efficient in temperatures around seventy-five degrees, give or take five degrees. Lower temperatures will slow the process. Higher temperatures hasten the fermentation.

One can always tell if fermentation is occurring. The presence of gas bubbles in the brine is the sign. Any pickles fermented in sealed barrels or kegs will need a hole to allow these gases to escape. All fermenting vegetables must be well below the level of the brine,

NOTE: These are the basic steps in Fermentation Pickling. Recipes for specific vegetables may modify some of them—and, of course, you will have to consult a recipe for the exact ingredients, amounts and times for the vegetable, or combination you wish to pickle.

1. Clean and weigh the vegetables carefully—the weight will determine the amounts of other ingredients called for.

2. Mix brine according to recipe.

3. Put vegetables into barrel or crock and pour in brine.

4. Hold vegetables submerged with a weighted-down inner lid. A dinner plate or wooden disc works well. Brick, rock, or water-filled jar or plastic bag makes a good weight. Be sure there is at least 2 inches of brine above the inner lid.

5. Remove scum from brine surface and scum ring from sides of container *daily,* leaving inner lid and weight in place.

submerged by the inner lid. Containers can be topped up by new brine of the original strength. Air is the villain for both the vegetables and brine, so be sure that there is at least a two inch brine covering over the weight. Remove all scum daily from the brine surfaces and container sides—this is the work of unwanted bacteria.

Once fermentation has stopped, in weeks or months depending on the recipe, there are several ways to preserve the pickles. Now that you've come this far it's a shame to lose anything to spoilage. It's the army of airborne organisms that once again must be defeated.

Pickles fermented in sealed barrels or kegs should have their gas-escape holes plugged. Be *sure* fermentation has ceased or there will be popping plugs in the night.

Large uncovered kegs, barrels and crocks should have final scum removed from all surface areas. They should then be sealed over with paraffin to prevent spoilage. Simply melt paraffin wax made for canning (available at the grocery store) in a nice clean coffee or fruit can. Pour a ⅛ inch thick layer over the top, pouring close to the surface to prevent air bubbles from forming. (If any bubbles occur, simply prick them with a fork to form an even layer.) Make sure paraffin touches all sides of the container. After wax is hardened, cover with a second layer of melted paraffin.

If you see bubbles after you've paraffined don't be alarmed. Simply break all the paraffin away and when you're sure that fermentation has indeed stopped, reparaffin.

Pickles made in large containers can also be transferred to smaller jars (by the way, there's no reason why you can't ferment in smaller jars right from the beginning). Pack the new hot, sterile jars with food; then top with brine. The brine may be somewhat murky. If that bothers you strain it either through a fine sieve or filter paper, and bring it to a boil. Seal the jars and process according to the water bath chart on page 25.

6. When fermentation has *stopped*—there are no more bubbles and no more scum being formed—remove the last of the scum and the inner lid. Seal the brine surface with an ⅛- to ¼-inch layer of paraffin. Pour from close to the surface to prevent air bubbles being trapped beneath wax.

7. If bubbles are formed, prick them with a fork and reseal holes.

8. When first layer of paraffin has hardened add a second layer being sure the edges are especially well sealed.
Alternate: When fermentation has stopped you may seal vegetables with enough of the liquid to cover, in clean, sterilized mason jars and process in a boiling-water bath. See page 24.

9. Cover and store in a cool place.

10. To use break the paraffin and remove as many at a time as you need from the brine. Produce will last up to several months if it's kept submerged in the brine.

Heat processing

Any food that is not eaten when fresh will rot if not preserved. There are several ways to preserve food; pickling is only one method. The microorganisms already present in food, and teeming in the air around us, would rather dispose of your food for you. Unfortunately the meal can't be shared; if the wrong bacteria are flourishing in your food you could get seriously ill.

By no means are all bacteria bad. You couldn't have digested your last meal, for example, without the presence of bacteria in your stomach. The fermented pickle is also testimony to friendly bacteria having done their work.

Nor can all microorganisms be destroyed by common methods such as simply boiling in water. The secret in the processing of foods is to

Check rim for cracks and chips

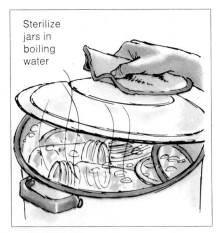

Sterilize jars in boiling water

control the growth of organisms already existing in the food and to make sure that no outsiders crash your pickling party.

All this is just a way of saying that, even though you're using preservatives like salt, there should be a step in the pickling procedure called heat processing. In this step the equipment and food will be given a bath in boiling water or in a steam pressure canner. Heat processing does not alter the flavor of pickles and assures extra safety in case something went wrong along the way.

The point of heat processing is to destroy bacteria by "cooking" the food *in the jar*. Pickles may be put into jars either hot or cold. Cold packing is best for foods such as tomatoes, peaches and other pickles that tend to float in liquid. Boiling syrup is then added to the food in the jars, completely covering the produce, leaving nothing exposed to air. Be sure to leave ¼ to ½ inch headspace between the top of the liquid or food product and the rim of the jar.

Leave head space when filling jars

¼" - ½"

Head space

Hot packing requires that food be boiled before it is placed in the jars. This is the method used for the majority of pickling products. Incidentally, hot packing shrinks the food somewhat and thus allows for more food to be packed per jar than with the cold method. Don't forget to leave ¼ to ½ inch headspace.

After the jars have been filled wipe the rims and screw on the lids firmly. The jars are now ready for the water bath.

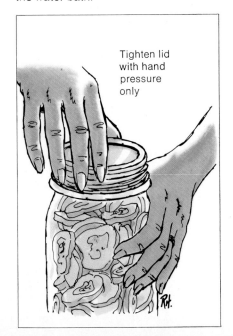

Tighten lid with hand pressure only

Canning jars, lids and rings are sterilized by placing them in a kettle of simmering water, bringing water to a boil and boiling steadily for 15 minutes.

Food can be heat processed in either a water bath, which is simply a large kettle, or in a steam-pressure cooker (steam canner). The water bath will heat food at two-hundred and twelve degrees, the temperature of boiling water. A steam canner cooks food at two-hundred and forty degrees, a temperature *absolutely essential* for processing certain meat products or other low acid and alkaline foods. It is in this latter type of food that the dangerous botulism organism thrives.

Most vegetables are low acid foods until the initial pickling steps are taken and vinegar raises their acid level. Most fruits are high acid foods. Meat is low acid and must be steam canned. Steam canners can be used for all heat processing chores though some picklers don't recommend them. The manufacturer's directions will supply you with specific information as to all foods and cooking times.

The common boiling water bath must provide at least an inch or more of water above the tops of the jars. Altitude is a determining factor (see chart) but the minimum duration of a water bath is five minutes. Be precise regarding times. It takes a while to kill bacteria but you want to avoid overcooking.

The heat processing, in addition to killing microorganisms, seals the jars airtight. One should understand the mechanics of that seal. When the caps are screwed on the filled jars the air pressure inside and out is equal. During the heating the contents of the jar expand, forcing air from the jar. When the jars are lifted from the boiling water, or the pressure released in the steam canner, there is an abrupt change for the jars and the lids are forced down by the stronger outside air pressure. As the jars' contents

Lift jar from water straight up using jar lifter

contract in the cooling process the relative pressure difference becomes even greater, creating a vacuum and thus eliminating air with its spoiling potential.

Be sure to lift the jars straight up out of the water bath. Do not tip the contents due to the risk of ruining the seal. Never open a jar to replace any lost liquid. Leave it sealed.

As an extra precaution some picklers advise an additional water bath, particularly for low acid foods, before eating. This is unnecessary for most pickles.

Testing the seal

Check the seals on all heat processed jars after twenty-four hours has elapsed. Remove the screw rims; the flat metal tops should be slightly depressed, sucked down, and they should be rigid. You should be able to lift the jar by the edges of the flat top alone. Roll the contents around

Press the lid to test the seal

the neck of the jar to check for leakage. There should be no "give" when you press the top of the flat lid.

Check the seals periodically. If imperfect seals are discovered the food in those jars must be water-bathed again. If too long a time has passed to salvage it, the food must be discarded without having been tasted.

Storing pickled products

Don't store any pickled product until you have checked the seals. If something has not sealed, either repeat the boiling water bath or place the jar in the refrigerator and use the product as soon as possible.

Jars should be stored in cool, dark, dry places. After opening, all pickle jars should be kept refrigerated, with the pickling liquid covering the fruits or vegetables.

You may refrigerate any small batches of pickled products such as fish, meats, vegetable, or fruit pickles, thereby eliminating the heat processing step. These refrigerated pickles must be used up within a few days or weeks. If you have any question about it being good, throw it out without tasting.

Boiling-water-bath time guide

Begin time count when water returns to boil after jars are immersed. Difference in chutney processing time depends upon ingredients used. (Based on USDA recommendations)

Product	Processing Time	Size of Container
Bread and butter pickles	10 minutes 5 minutes	Quart Pint
Chutneys	5-20 minutes	Pint
Dills, fermented	15 minutes	Quart
Dills, unfermented	20 minutes	Quart
Fruit pickles	20 minutes	Pint
Gherkins	5 minutes	Pint
Green beans	5 minutes	Pint
Melon rinds	5 minutes	Pint
Relish, tomato, pepper or onion	5 minutes	Pint
Relish, corn	15 minutes	Pint
Sauerkraut	15 minutes	Quart
Sliced cucumbers	5 minutes	Pint

Water bath altitude conversion chart

Increase water bath canner time by indicated minutes if the time called for is:

Altitude in feet	20 Minutes or less	More than 30 minutes
1,000	1	2
2,000	2	4
3,000	3	6
4,000	4	8
5,000	5	10
6,000	6	12
7,000	7	14
8,000	8	16
9,000	9	18
10,000	10	20

Altitude chart

Pressure Canner

Altitude	Process at:	
Sea level—2,000 feet	10	pounds
2,000— 3,000 feet	11½	pounds
3,000— 4,000 feet	12	pounds
4,000— 5,000 feet	12½	pounds
5,000— 6,000 feet	13	pounds
6,000— 7,000 feet	13½	pounds
7,000— 8,000 feet	14	pounds
8,000— 9,000 feet	14½	pounds
9,000—10,000 feet	15	pounds

A peck of pickled peppers...

All-American favorites and samples of international cuisine. Collected recipes for pickled vegetables, edible ornamentals, fruits, nuts, eggs, meats and fish. Plus serving and gift suggestions.

The recipes in this book have been carefully chosen to give you many different pickling experiences. Some are so quick and easy they'll seem like child's play. In fact we're sure many young picklers will enjoy using our handbook.

A few recipes may seem long and time-consuming at first reading. But when you consider that the procedures are spread out over a long time span, requiring only minutes each day, then they, too, become easy to do.

We've offered a few unusual ways of pickling to contrast with our American standbys. Try some of the Japanese, Chinese, Korean and Indian delicacies. The Scandinavians perform miracles in pickling fish which you'll surely want to try. Other European countries lend their ideas along with some delightful Middle Eastern condiments. There are even recipes from other sections of our country which may be new to you.

Vegetable pickle recipes are categorized alphabetically by types, with various pickling suggestions under each. For example, if you have a large supply of beets, turn to our beet section and you'll find several ways of turning them into pickled products —from russel to relish. A section on

Preceding page
A cool, dark, dry pantry is well-stocked with many of the hundreds of pickled products found within these pages.

mixed vegetables begins on page 56, highlighted by quite a number of relish combinations.

Fruit pickling begins with the making of chutney on page 60. We feel sure you will find some new ideas for fruits you never thought of turning into pickles.

Try something new. We've given a few suggestions merely as a point of departure.

Our section on pickled meats and fish may be among the most interesting with some tasty recipes that are fun to prepare and serve.

And speaking of serving, our charts on pages 88 and 89 will give you ideas as to what-to-serve, when and how.

Pickle recipe guidelines

Use today's pickle recipes. Many of the older recipes will not be as successful as they were 25 years ago. At that time vinegar had less acetic acid than it does now, so you may find your recipe will call for too much vinegar. Follow up-to-date directions backed by research. We strongly advise a thorough reading of the previous two portions of this book, both for the veteran pickler and the novice.

As with any other type of cooking, don't start a pickling process until you have thoroughly read the recipe, assembled all the equipment and have both equipment and produce properly prepared. Then work quickly, to preserve the "freshness" of your pickles.

Don't bite off more than you can chew by trying to prepare more of any pickle product than you can handle carefully and enjoyably in a single process.

In many of our recipes we do not attempt to estimate a yield, since the size of fruits and vegetables vary. All cooking temperature degrees are given in fahrenheit.

Some of our recipes will give you an estimated waiting time before using a product. Others indicate that the pickle is ready for immediate use. In most cases it's best to allow several weeks to elapse before opening the jar so flavors can fully develop.

The first time you try a recipe it is advisable to follow proportions exactly and make only a small batch to test the flavor. Then if you find it not to your liking, you haven't wasted a lot of time or foodstuff. Also you'll have an idea of what to add, subtract or increase to meet your family's taste requirements.

Artichokes

The edible portion of this plant is the flower bud. Harvest mature buds just prior to spreading of the bud scales. Whole immature buds can also be harvested for pickling. At least 1½ inches of stem should be included. Artichoke hearts or bottoms are available canned or frozen where fresh ones are not available.

Pickled Artichokes in Oil

48 to 52 small artichokes (about 3-inch diameter) or 72 to 78 artichoke hearts
2½ teaspoons citric acid or
  1 cup lemon juice
2 quarts of water
  White distilled vinegar
1 clove garlic per pint
2 bay leaves per pint
¼ teaspoon sweet basil per pint
¼ teaspoon oregano per pint
1 cup olive oil and 3 cups salad oil
  or 4 cups olive oil

1. Use small artichokes or artichoke hearts. Pull off outer leaves. Cut off top of bud and trim stem. Wash thoroughly.

2. Add artichokes to a solution of citric acid or lemon juice and water. Bring to a boil and simmer small hearts 3 minutes; mature hearts 5 minutes; and small, whole artichokes 10 minutes.

3. Drain artichokes and place in sterilized pint jars. Cover with vinegar and let stand 10 to 14 hours. Drain and cover with fresh vinegar. Allow to stand for an additional 4 hours.

4. Drain. Add spices to each jar and fill with oil. Seal. Process in boiling water bath 30 minutes.
(Makes 4 pints)

Pickled Artichokes in Wine Vinegar

1. Follow steps 1 and 2 for "Pickled Artichokes in Oil."

2. Drain artichokes. Place in pint jars. Cover with white distilled vinegar and let stand 10 to 14 hours.

3. Drain. Add spices, and cover with white wine vinegar. Pack in sterilized pint jars. Seal. Process in boiling water bath 20 minutes.
(Makes 4 pints)

Asparagus

The aristocrat of vegetables does not produce an abundant harvest until the third season after planting. Gourmet "white asparagus" spears are achieved by mounding soil around the developing spear to shield it from sunlight. Asparagus pickles are delicately flavored.

Tender asparagus spears are alternated with strips of sweet red peppers. Artichoke hearts are pickled, then preserved in oil and herbs.

Beans and other legumes

Green beans are easy-to-grow, easy-to-find commercially and easy-to-pickle. Mix green and wax beans for color interest. Dried beans and other legumes lend themselves more to quick marinations or sauces. Sprouted beans can be added to pickled Oriental vegetables.

Dilly Beans

4 pounds green beans
6 tablespoons salt
3 cups distilled white vinegar
3 cups water
1 tablespoon dill seed or fresh dill
1 tablespoon mustard seed
18 whole black peppercorns or 1½ teaspoons dried hot red peppers, seeds removed and pepper crushed

1. Wash beans thoroughly and cut in small pieces, or use whole small beans.

2. Combine salt, vinegar, and water. Heat to boiling point.

3. Pack beans into hot, sterilized jars. Add to each jar ½ teaspoon dill seed or fresh dill head, ½ teaspoon mustard seed and 3 whole peppercorns, or ¼ teaspoon hot red peppers. Pour boiling liquid over beans. Seal.

4. Process in boiling water for 20 minutes. (Makes 6 to 7 pints)

Pickled String-Beans

6 pounds string-beans
4 cups water
2 tablespoons cinnamon
2 teaspoons whole cloves
2 teaspoons whole allspice
4 cups distilled white vinegar
4 cups sugar
2 lemons, sliced thin

1. Snip ends off beans and parboil in small amount of boiling salted water about 6 minutes.

2. Drain beans and combine with all other ingredients: simmer about 15 minutes.

3. Pack beans in hot, sterilized jars. Fill with liquid and seal. Process 5 minutes. (Makes 4 quarts)

Mixed Beans

½ cup distilled white vinegar
½ cup sugar
½ cup safflower or olive oil
2 cups cooked green beans
2 cups cooked wax beans
2 cups cooked kidney beans
1 sliced sweet white or red onion
½ cup chopped sweet pepper
½ cup chopped celery
1 tablespoon fresh basil or ¾ teaspoon dried

1. Mix vinegar, sugar and oil, stirring until sugar is dissolved.

Young Asparagus Pickle

4 pounds very thin green asparagus
2 onions, sliced very thin
2 red bell peppers, cut in julienne strips (seeds removed)
2 teaspoons salt
5 cups cider vinegar
3 tablespoons sugar
3 tablespoons mixed pickling spices
2 cups water

1. Wash the asparagus thoroughly in cold water. Lay the onions neatly on the bottoms of two 1-quart jars. Pack the asparagus cut end down with the red pepper strips to give a striped effect to the filled bottles.

2. Boil the remaining ingredients for 10 minutes, then fill jars with hot mixture. Seal. Process 20 minutes. (Makes 2 quarts)

Pickled White Asparagus

6 pounds white asparagus, peeled
3 cups distilled white vinegar
2 tablespoons salt
2 tablespoons sugar
2 cups water
1 tablespoon mustard seed
1 tablespoon white peppercorns
3 cloves garlic, peeled
3 bay leaves

1. Parboil asparagus just until barely tender, about 3 to 5 minutes, depending on the thickness. Pack it, cut end down neatly into hot sterilized quart jars.

2. Boil the remaining ingredients together 10 minutes. Remove garlic and bay leaves putting one of each in each jar. Pour the liquid over the asparagus and seal. Process 20 minutes. (Makes 3 quarts)

2. Combine remaining ingredients. Pour liquid over.

3. Cover and chill. Let marinate at least 12 hours. If desired seal and process large quantities 5 minutes.

Mississippi Relish

- 1 cup dried black-eyed peas, soaked overnight
  Small piece ham-hock
  Salt to taste
- ¼ cup distilled white vinegar
- ⅔ cup salad oil
- 1 clove garlic, finely minced
- ¼ cup sugar
- 1 tablespoon fresh oregano or ¾ teaspoon dried
- 2 teaspoons fresh basil or ½ teaspoon dried
- 2 teaspoons freshly ground pepper

1. Cook peas with ham-hock, drain.

2. Mix remaining ingredients well and pour over warm peas.

3. Cover and chill overnight. Use within a few days.

Three Marinades for Legumes

(Garbanzo beans, lentils, red kidney beans, lima beans, fava beans, etc.)

I. Dilled Marinade

- 1 cup olive oil
- 3 tablespoons lemon juice
- ½ teaspoon salt
- ½ teaspoon freshly ground black pepper
- ½ cup chopped fresh dill

II. Mustard Marinade

- 1 cup white wine vinegar
- 2 teaspoons sugar
- ½ teaspoon salt
- ¼ cup olive oil
- ½ cup minced onion
- 2 tablespoons chopped fresh parsley
- 1 tablespoon chopped fresh tarragon
- ¼ teaspoon white pepper
- 1 teaspoon dry mustard
- 2 teaspoons chopped capers

III. Spicy Marinade

- 1 cup olive oil
- ¼ cup red wine vinegar
- 2 cloves garlic, minced
- 2 tablespoons minced onion
- 2 tablespoons chopped fresh basil
- 2 anchovy fillets, mashed to paste or 1 teaspoon salt
- 1 teaspoon dried oregano
- 1 teaspoon freshly ground black pepper
- 2 teaspoons chopped parsley

The legumes should be refrigerated in the marinade at least 24 hours, but are much better after several days. Keep them in covered containers.

The flavor of fresh dill blends with mixed green and wax beans in our "Dilly Bean" recipe (page 29).

Beets

These prolific vegetables lend themselves to pickling in all stages of development from tiny immature sizes pickled whole to mature sizes sliced or chopped fine for relishes. Beets are ready for harvest in about 6 to 7 weeks from seed. The newer golden beets make delicious pickles, but the color is not very appetizing.

Beet Pickles

- 2 cups sugar
- 1 tablespoon whole allspice
- 1½ teaspoons salt
- 2 sticks cinnamon
- 3½ cups distilled white vinegar
- 1½ cups water
- 3 quarts small beets

1. Wash beets. Leave roots and 2 inches of stems so they won't bleed. Cook until tender, slip skins and trim off stems.

2. Combine the rest of the ingredients. Simmer 15 minues.

3. Pack beets into clean hot jars. (Cut larger beets in half.)

4. Bring liquid back to boiling and pour over beets. Seal. Process in boiling water bath 30 minutes.

Note: If you have only enough beets for a pint or two, save the pickling liquid in the refrigerator until more beets are available.

Russel (Beet Sour)

- 12 pounds beets
  Water

1. Put beets, peeled and quartered, into a 12-quart crock. Cover them with water and cover the crock. Set crock in a warm place.

2. After 1 week remove the white foam which will have formed on the surface of the water, then stir the beets.

3. Repeat step #2 twice more at weekly intervals. The Russel is ready in about 24 days.
(Makes about 12 pints)

Russel Borsht

The traditional way to serve russel.

- 6 cups russel
- ⅓ cup sugar
- 2 onions, chopped
- 2 eggs, beaten
- 3 hard-boiled eggs, peeled and chopped
- 1 cucumber, peeled and chopped
- 2 tablespoons chopped parsley
- 3 hot, boiled, medium-sized potatoes, peeled and diced

1. Boil russel with sugar and onions for 12 minutes.

2. Strain the russel and let it cool slightly, then stir in the beaten eggs.

3. Stir in the rest of the ingredients and ladle into bowls. (Serves 6)

Spiced Beets

- 2 cups cider vinegar
- 2 cups water
- 1 teaspoon salt
- 2 cups sugar
- 1 tablespoon mustard seed
- 1 teaspoon whole allspice
- 1 teaspoon whole cloves
- 3 cinnamon sticks
- 4 pounds small beets, peeled
- 1 pound onions, thinly sliced

1. Combine vinegar, water, salt, sugar and spices in a large pot and boil 5 minutes.

2. Add beets and onions and simmer 15 minutes.

3. Pour beets and brine into quart jars and seal. Process 30 minutes. (Makes 3 quarts)

Beet Relish

- 4 cups coarsely ground raw beets
- 6 cups coarsely ground cabbage
- 2 cups coarsely ground onions
- 2 cups sugar
- 2 tablespoons horseradish, freshly grated or bottled
- 1 tablespoon salt
- 2 cups distilled white vinegar

1. Combine all ingredients in a large kettle.

2. Bring to a boil. Cook until thick, about 20 minutes, stirring occasionally.

3. Pack hot into hot, sterilized jars. Seal.

4. Process in boiling water for 20 minutes. (Makes 4 to 5 pints)

Broccoli

Harvest when buds are about the size of a matchead before the flowers show yellow color. Especially good in mixed vegetable pickles and marinations.

Pickled Broccoli with Tarragon

- 3 pounds broccoli, flowerets and sliced, peeled stalks
- Brine: ½ cup salt to 2 quarts water
- 3 cups white wine vinegar
- 1 cup water
- ¼ cup salt
- 3 tablespoons mixed pickling spices
- 1 bunch (about 3 ounces) fresh tarragon or 2 tablespoons dried
- 1 tablespoon peppercorns

1. Soak broccoli in brine overnight.

2. Rinse thoroughly and pack into hot, sterilized jars.

3. Boil remaining ingredients for 10 minutes and pour over broccoli, filling jars and making sure to distribute the tarragon equally among the jars. Seal. Process 20 minutes. (Makes 2 pints)

Italian Pickled Broccoli

1 quart cider vinegar
1½ cups water
3 tablespoons mixed pickling spice
1½ tablespoons fresh oregano or
    1¼ teaspoons dried
2 tablespoons fresh basil or
    2 teaspoons dried
1 tablespoon black peppercorns
6 cloves garlic, slivered
1 cup sugar
5 pounds broccoli, flowerets and
    peeled stalks, quartered and cut
    in 1½ inch sections
2 red bell peppers, seeded and
    coarsely chopped
2 large onions, sliced

1. In a large kettle combine the vinegar, water, spices, herbs and sugar. Bring to a boil and simmer 15 minutes

2. Add vegetables and boil 8 to 10 minutes, or until broccoli is just tender.

3. Pack into hot, sterilized jars and seal. Process 20 minutes. (Makes 4 pints)

Brussels sprouts

A delectable fall and winter vegetable that can be adapted to many of the cabbage recipes for marination or spicing.

Brussels Sprouts Pickle

Salt—to taste
6 pounds Brussels sprouts, cleaned
    and halved
2 quarts white wine vinegar
1 cup brown sugar, packed
½ cup mustard seed
Spice bag:
    2 tablespoons whole cloves
    2 nutmegs, broken in pieces
    2 tablespoons whole allspice
    3 tablespoons black peppercorns
    2 tablespoons celery seed
    5 bay leaves, broken into pieces

1. Salt the sprouts and let stand overnight in a cool place. Next day rinse them thoroughly in cold water and drain.

2. Pack in hot, sterilized jars.

3. Combine remaining ingredients in a pot and boil 10 minutes. Remove spice bag and pour liquid over the sprouts, filling jars with more vinegar if necessary. Seal. Process 15 minutes. (Makes 5 pints)

Green and White Pickle

1 quart cider vinegar
2 cups water
3 tablespoons salt
1 cup sugar
Spice bag:
    1 tablespoon black peppercorns
    4 bay leaves
    2 tablespoons mustard seed
    2 tablespoons celery seed
    3 sprigs tarragon, crushed

2 tablespoons whole cloves
4 cloves garlic, peeled
2 pounds whole Brussels sprouts,
    washed and trimmed
2 pounds small white onions, peeled

1. Combine vinegar, water, salt, sugar and spice bag in large pot. Bring to boil and simmer for 15 minutes.

2. Add vegetables and cook gently 10 minutes or until onions turn translucent.

3. Remove spice bag. Pack onions and sprouts into hot, sterilized jars.

4. Fill jars with hot vinegar mixture and seal. Process 15 minutes. (Makes 3 pints)

Cabbage

The mention of pickled cabbage immediately brings sauerkraut to mind. In addition to this nutritious delicacy there are many other ways of pickling cabbage year-round.

Spiced Cabbage

4 quarts shredded cabbage
½ cup coarse salt
1 quart cider vinegar
1½ cups sugar
1 tablespoon mustard seed
1 tablespoon ground fresh horseradish
1 teaspoon whole cloves
4 cinnamon sticks, broken

1. Layer the cabbage and salt in a crock overnight. Next day press out all the juice and rinse.

2. In a saucepan boil vinegar with sugar, mustard seed, and horseradish. Put the spices in a cheesecloth bag and add to pot. Simmer 15 minutes.

3. Pack the cabbage into hot, sterilized pint jars and fill with spiced vinegar. Seal and process for 20 minutes. (Makes 4 pints)

Pickled Red Cabbage

2 small red cabbages (3 pounds)
⅓ cup coarse salt
1 quart cider vinegar
3 whole cloves
½ teaspoon ground nutmeg
2 bay leaves
2 tablespoons mixed pickling spices
2 tablespoons sugar

1. Quarter the cabbages, remove the stems and cores and shred cabbage.

2. Mix cabbage and salt in a bowl and refrigerate 2 days.

3. Drain cabbage, squeeze it dry and pack it into hot, sterilized jars.

4. Boil the remaining ingredients as long as brine covers top and it is well and pack into hot, sterilized jars. covering the cabbage. Seal. Process 20 minutes. (Makes 4 pints)

Sauerkraut

Sauerkraut—acid cabbage—results from a curing process in which many bacteria appear on the cut edges of cabbage. The added salt draws out the natural sugar stored in the vegetable. Some of the present bacteria act upon the sugar, changing it to acids, thus resulting in a mellowing of the cabbage.

1½ teaspoons salt to each 1 pound
    cabbage

1. Choose large, firm, well-ripened cabbage. Allow heads to stand at room temperature for about 24 hours to wilt. (Causes leaves to become less brittle, therefore less likely to break when cutting.)

2. Trim away outer leaves and wash heads; cut into quarters or halves. Remove core or cut fine. Shred cabbage with a sharp knife or with kraut-cutter which has blades set to shred about the thickness of a dime.

3. Weigh the shredded cabbage and add proper proportion of salt. Mix together in a large enameled, stainless steel, or aluminum pot. Let the salted cabbage stand for 3 to 5 minutes before packing.

4. Place in a crock or paraffined barrel. Press gently, but firmly, with hands or wooden spoon to release brine. Continue filling. Brine continues to form for 24 hours.

5. Place a piece of plastic or clean, white, thin cloth over top and tuck inside. Place a fitted top inside the crock. Or use a heavy, weighted plate or heavy duty plastic bag filled with water to keep the cabbage immersed.

6. Let cabbage stand in crock at room temperature for about two weeks. If the temperature is very cool the process may take as long as five to six weeks. Remove scum from surface daily, wash cloth or plastic and replace weight.

7. Sauerkraut is complete when bubbles stop rising to the surface, although fermentation continues. Taste to check flavor during process. When kraut suits your taste, remove from crock. Heat to simmering and pack into hot, sterilized jars. If there is not enough cabbage liquid, heat 1½ tablespoons salt to 1 quart water. Pour into jars, leaving half-inch head space.

8. Seal and process in boiling-water bath, allowing 20 minutes for quarts, 15 minutes for pints.

Notes: A 3-gallon crock holds 24 pounds of cut cabbage.

Carrots and purple cabbage blended in "Raw Carrot Relish" (page 36).

Sauerkraut is the perfect complement to the spicy flavor of smoked sausages. It's easy and fun to make in quantity or small batches.
1. Shred or cut cabbage quarters with a kraut cutter or sharp French knife. **2.** Weigh the cabbage. **3.** Add correct ratio of salt.
(See page 33.) **4.** Mix well with hands or wooden spoons. **5.** Place in a crock and gently press down with hands, wooden spoon, or mallet to start the juices flowing. **6.** Weight down with a lid or plate that fits inside crock. Top with a heavy object, such as a jar of water, to keep cabbage submerged below brine surface. **7.** Leave in brine until fermentation stops or until desired degree of tartness is reached. Then drain and serve, store in crock, or pack into jars for processing.

If kraut will all be eaten in a few months, it can be stored in the crock, as long as brine covers top and it is kept cool.

For illustrated step-by-step procedures, see page 35.

Carrots

These versatile vitamin storehouses can be pickled in early immature stages. It's an easy one for beginning picklers.

Golden Nuggets

2 pounds fresh carrots, sliced and cooked
1 medium-sized green pepper, cut into thin slices, seeds removed
2 green onions, cut into thick slices
1 cup tomato sauce
¼ cup oil
¾ cup sugar
¾ cup cider vinegar
1 teaspoon prepared mustard
1 teaspoon Worcestershire sauce

1. Combine all ingredients.

2. Let stand in refrigerator 24 hours.

3. Place in pint jars. Seal and process 15 minutes.

Pickled cauliflower flowerets (recipe above) are grouped in a ceramic lettuce leaf bowl to reconstruct a cauliflower head.

Raw Carrot Relish

10 carrots, peeled (6 cups)
3 large green peppers, seeded (3 cups)
3 large red bell peppers, seeded (3 cups)
1 large head red cabbage (6 cups)
3 medium-sized onions, peeled (3 cups)
6 cups white wine vinegar
2 cups sugar
3 tablespoons salt
1 tablespoon mustard seed
1 tablespoon celery seed
1 tablespoon allspice

1. Put all the vegetables through the coarse blade of a food chopper. Mix well and pack into hot, sterilized jars. Color may be dark. The hot vinegar will restore good color.

2. Mix the vinegar with remaining ingredients in a saucepan. Bring the mixture to a boil and simmer 10 minutes.

3. Pour the boiling vinegar mixture over the vegetables, covering completely.

4. Cover jars. Store in the refrigerator. (Makes 4 quarts)

Cauliflower

Many people prefer pickled cauliflower to any other way of preparation. It's great by itself or mixed with other vegetable pickles. Harvest when heads are compact and fairly smooth and white.

Pickled Cauliflower

4 pounds cauliflowerets
12 medium onions, peeled and sliced
¼ cup salt
1 small dried hot red pepper, seeds removed
½ teaspoon whole cloves
¾ cup sugar
1 teaspoon ground turmeric
2 teaspoons whole mustard seed
1 teaspoon whole celery seed
1½ cups white vinegar
1½ cups water

1. Salt (to taste) the vegetables and let stand overnight. On the next day rinse them with cold water several times.

2. Place the red pepper and cloves in a cheesecloth bag. Combine with the remaining ingredients and boil for 5 minutes.

3. Add the vegetables and cook just until they begin to lose their crispness about 5-10 minutes. Do not overcook.

4. Discard the bag of red pepper and cloves and pack the pickle into hot, sterilized jars. Fill the jars with the liquid and seal. Process 15 minutes. (Makes 7 pints)

Spiced Pickled Cauliflower

1 quart vinegar
1 cup sugar
2 tablespoons mustard seed
10 whole cloves
4 cinnamon sticks
8 whole allspice
1 nutmeg, broken
2 heads cauliflower, cleaned and broken into flowerets

1. Simmer the vinegar, sugar and spices for 15 minutes.

2. Blanch cauliflower by plunging it into boiling water, turning off heat, and letting stand 2 minutes.

3. Drain the vegetable and pack into jars.

4. Strain the hot syrup into the jars, covering the cauliflower. Seal at once. Process 15 minutes. (Makes 3 quarts)

P'ao Ts'ai (Chinese cauliflower pickle)

1 large cauliflower, cut up
½ cabbage, chopped coarsely
1 cucumber, seeded and chopped
3 green peppers, seeded and cut into 1-inch squares
3 hot red chili peppers, seeds removed
1 carrot, peeled and diced
2 cups distilled white vinegar
½ cup sugar
1 teaspoon salt

1. Boil cauliflower in a large pot for 10 minutes, drain off water and add remaining vegetables and chilies.

2. In another pot boil the vinegar, sugar and salt. Pour over vegetables and let stand 5 hours covered. The pickle may be served at once, or refrigerate in a covered jar. (Makes 2 quarts)

Middle-Eastern Pickled Cauliflower

1 large head cauliflower
1 cup vinegar
2 cups water
2 teaspoons salt
1 small beet, cooked and chopped

1. Wash cauliflower and cut into flowerets. Cook in boiling salted water until just barely tender; drain.

2. Make a brine of vinegar, water and salt. Pour over vegetables and pack into hot, sterilized jars. Seal. Process 15 minutes. Pickle is ready in a week. (Makes 2 pints)

Celery

A year-round available vegetable that is usually pickled along with mixed vegetable medleys. Here the celery is in the spotlight.

When pickled in immature stages tomatoes, corn and eggplant appear as miniatures of the mature vegetable.

Celery Relish

2 green peppers, seeded and chopped
2 sweet red peppers, seeded and chopped
6 medium-sized onions, chopped
2 quarts sliced celery, cut into ½-inch pieces
3 tablespoons salt
1¼ cups sugar
3 tablespoons mustard seed
1 teaspoon turmeric
⅔ cup light corn syrup
1⅔ cups distilled white vinegar
⅔ cup water

1. Combine all the ingredients in a large covered kettle. Bring the mixture to a boil and simmer for 3 to 5 minutes, or until vegetables are crisp-tender.

2. Pack into hot, sterilized jars, making sure that the liquid covers the vegetables. Seal. Process 15 minutes. (Makes about 5 pints)

Corn

Harvested in "miniature" stages, corn is a conversation piece on the condiment tray. Harvested at the "milk stage" it can be transformed into a superior relish.

Corn Relish

18 medium-sized ears of corn (2 quarts corn kernels)
2 cups chopped red bell pepper, seeds removed
2 cups chopped green bell pepper, seeds removed
1 quart chopped celery
1 cup chopped onion
1 cup sugar
1 quart distilled white vinegar
2 tablespoons salt
2 teaspoons celery seed
2 tablespoons dry mustard
1 teaspoon turmeric
¼ cup all-purpose flour
½ cup water

1. Place corn-on-the-cob in boiling salted water and simmer for 5 minutes. Dip in cold water.

2. Drain and cut kernels from cob. Do not scrape.

3. Combine next 8 ingredients in a large pot. Simmer 15 minutes.

4. Mix mustard, turmeric, and flour with water. Add with corn to pepper mixture.

5. Simmer 5 minutes, stirring constantly.

6. Pack into hot, sterilized jars, seal and process 10 minutes in boiling water bath. (Makes about 7 pints)

Pickled Miniature Vegetables

You may use either miniature ears of corn, baby carrots, baby avocados, baby eggplants, tiny cucumbers, chive bulbs or onions for this recipe.

1 quart miniature vegetable, selected from above list
Water
3 cups distilled white vinegar
1 cup sugar
3 tablespoons mixed pickling spices, tied in a cheesecloth bag

1. Cook the vegetable in water until it is half tender. (Time will vary according to type of vegetable)

2. Boil the vinegar with the sugar, spices and ½ cup water for 10 minutes. Take out the spices.

3. Add the vegetable and boil a few minutes more, until almost tender.

4. Pack the vegetable in hot, sterilized jars and pour the liquid over it filling the bottles. Seal. Process 10 minutes. (Makes 2 pints)

Cucumbers

Cucumbers and pickles are synonymous. Many picklers specialize in this vegetable. Here are some time-honored methods as well as a few "new" ideas for your cucumber "harvest." Be sure to select from "pickling" varieties. See page 4. Differences in fermenting processes and fresh-pack methods are explained on pages 18-23.

Harkema Dill Pickles

3 quarts water
1 quart cider vinegar
½ cup salt
5 pounds small pickling cucumbers
Sprigs of dill
½ teaspoon minced garlic
½ teaspoon mixed pickling spices

1. Bring first 3 ingredients to a boil.

2. Scrub cucumbers thoroughly with a brush in cool water.

3. Pack in jars and add the spices.

4. Pour boiling liquid over the cucumbers and seal.

5. Process 20 minutes.

Agnes Carter's Mother's Dill Pickles

"This recipe is from Agnes Carter's mother. I've done my dills this way for over 15 years—we like it so well I haven't dared change. I've rarely had a jar go bad and if one starts to turn cloudy, I put it in the refrigerator and use it or pour off the old brine and make new."

6 pounds small pickling cucumbers
Fresh dill
Garlic
3 quarts water
3 cups vinegar
¾ cup salt
¾ teaspoon alum

1. Scrub fresh cucumbers under running water, remove blossom end, dry and pack in sterilized jars with top and stalk of fresh dill and 1 or 2 cloves garlic.

2. Combine water, vinegar, salt and alum and bring to a boil. Pour over the cucumbers and seal. Process 20 minutes.

3. Pickles are ready in approximately 4 to 8 weeks.

Note: For variety add 1 hot pepper per jar or 1 teaspoon mustard seed.

Ethel Sell's Kosher Dills

1 quart water
1 pint vinegar
½ cup salt
3 pounds small pickling cucumbers

1. Bring water, vinegar and salt to a boil and remove from heat. Pack fresh cucumbers in sterilized jars.

To each quart jar add:

2 large heads dill
2 teaspoons mixed pickling spices
2 small red hot pepper pods, seeds removed
2 cloves garlic

2. Pour liquid over slowly, fill jars and seal.

3. Process in boiling-water bath 20 minutes for quarts. Pickles are ready in 6 to 8 weeks.

Quick Dill Pickles

4 pounds or 2 quarts of cucumbers
6 tablespoons salt
3 cups vinegar
3 cups water
Dill seed or fresh heads dill weed
Mixed pickling spices
Black peppercorns

1. Wash cucumbers thoroughly.

2. For whole cucumbers, small sizes up to 4 inches are preferred. Larger sizes may be packed whole provided they are processed for a longer time. Usually with larger cucumbers it is better to slice, quarter, or halve lengthwise before pickling.

3. Combine salt, vinegar and water. Heat to boiling.

4. Pack cucumbers into hot, sterilized jars. For each pint jar, add 1 teaspoon dill seed or 1 head dill, 1½ teaspoons mixed pickling spices and 3 black peppercorns.

5. Fill with boiled vinegar-salt solution to ½ inch of top for quarts or ¼ inch for pints.

6. Process large whole cucumbers in boiling water allowing 10 minutes for pint jars and 20 minutes for quarts. Process small whole cucumbers, slices, halves, or quarters in boiling water allowing 5 minutes for pint jars and 10 minutes for quarts. (Makes 6 pints)

Sweet Dill Chunks

12 large dill pickles prepared by the "Quick Dill" method or use commercially-packed pickles
4 cloves garlic
2 teaspoons mixed pickling spices
4 cups sugar
2 cups distilled white vinegar

1. Cut dill pickles into chunks and pack into sterilized jars.

2. Add 1 clove garlic and ½ teaspoon mixed pickling spices to each jar.

3. Combine sugar and vinegar and bring to a boil.

4. Pour over pickles and seal. Process 5 minutes. (Makes 4 pints)

Kosher-Style Dill Pickles

Follow recipe for "Quick Dill Pickles," except in step 5, add 2 cloves garlic, peeled and halved, to each jar.

Sweet Cucumber Pickles

7 pounds thinly sliced cucumbers
2 gallons water
2 cups pickling lime
8 cups distilled white vinegar
9 cups sugar
1 tablespoon salt
1 teaspoon whole cloves
1 teaspoon celery seed
1 teaspoon mixed pickling spices

1. Soak cucumbers in water and lime for 24 hours.

2. Wash in clean water and soak in fresh water for 3 hours.

3. Combine remaining ingredients, add cucumbers and soak overnight.

4. Boil pickles in soaking liquid until pickles are clear (approximately 1 hour).

5. Pour into hot, sterilized jars. Seal. Process 5 minutes. (Makes 7 pints)

Chunk Pickles

25 large, or about 6 pounds, cucumbers
3¼ cups salt
3 quarts water
2 tablespoons alum
1 quart distilled white vinegar
8 cups sugar
2 two-inch stick cinnamon
2 blades mace
1 tablespoon whole cloves

1. Wash cucumbers; place in stone crock or jar; cover with cold brine made by dissolving salt in water; let stand 2 weeks.

2. Remove cucumbers from brine; wash; trim off stem ends; cut crosswise into 1-inch pieces.

3. Cover with cold water; add alum; let stand overnight. Drain; wash well.

4. Combine remaining ingredients. Bring to boil. Pour immediately over cucumber chunks; let stand.

5. Drain syrup, bring to boil and pour over, repeating process three successive days.

6. Fourth day, place cucumbers in jars, and pour over hot syrup. Seal. Process 5 minutes. (Makes 8 pints)

Mustard Pickles

1 quart small green tomatoes
4 red bell peppers
1 quart small pickling onions
2 quarts small cucumbers
1 head cauliflower
2 cups salt
1 gallon cold water
1 cup all-purpose flour
6 tablespoons dry mustard
1 cup sugar
1 tablespoon turmeric
Distilled white vinegar

1. Cut tomatoes, peppers, cucumbers and cauliflower in medium pieces. Add onions.

2. Make brine of salt and water and pour over vegetables, let stand 24 hours. Heat just to scalding point, then drain.

3. Mix flour, mustard, sugar and turmeric with enough cold vinegar to make 2 quarts in all. Cook until thickened, stirring constantly.

4. Add pickles. Heat thoroughly and pour into sterilized, hot jars and seal. Process 10 minutes. (Makes 4 pints)

Amber Relish

12 cucumbers
6 white onions
½ cup salt
Water
1 quart distilled white vinegar
2 cups sugar
¼ teaspoon cinnamon
1 teaspoon mustard seed
1 teaspoon dry mustard
¼ teaspoon ground cloves
1 tablespoon turmeric

1. Peel and chop cucumbers and onions.

2. Add salt and enough water to cover. Let stand 1 hour. Drain off brine.

3. Boil vinegar, sugar and spices together for 20 minutes.

4. Add vegetables. Cook slowly until tender and all the ingredients have become yellow in color.

5. Pack into hot, sterilized jars. Seal. Process 5 minutes. (Makes 4 to 5 pints)

Oil Cucumber Pickles

2 quarts cucumbers, sliced (20 to 25) or 2 quarts very small cucumbers
½ cup salt
¼ cup whole mustard seed
½ teaspoon celery seed
⅛ teaspoon pepper
¼ cup sugar
¼ cup olive oil
3 cups distilled white vinegar

1. Arrange cucumbers in alternate layers with salt in a bowl. Cover with cold water and let stand overnight.

2. Drain and pack into sterilized jars.

3. Add spices, sugar and olive oil to vinegar. Bring to boil and pour over cucumbers. Seal. Process 5 minutes. (Makes 4 half-pints)

Sweet Baby Gherkins

6 dozen tiny immature cucumbers
Brine:
1 cup salt
¼ cup distilled vinegar
2 quarts water
Syrup:
1 stick cinnamon
1½ teaspoons whole cloves
1½ teaspoons mixed pickling spices
3 cups distilled white vinegar
6 cups sugar

1. For brine, bring salt, vinegar and water to boil. Cool and pour over cucumbers in a crock. Cover and let stand 2 weeks in a cool place. Remove scum daily.

2. Drain and discard brine. Cover cucumbers with cold water and let stand 24 hours. Rinse and drain.

3. Tie spices in cheesecloth bag. Place in a saucepan with vinegar and sugar. Bring to boil. Pour over cucumbers. Let stand 24 hours. Drain, reserving syrup.

4. Repeat draining and boiling process 3 times.

5. Pack in hot, sterilized jars. Seal. Process for 10 minutes in boiling water bath.

Cherry Pickles—Sweet

1 dozen 4-inch cucumbers
1 quart cherry or grape leaves
Distilled white vinegar
1 cup salt
½ gallon water
1½ cups sugar
2 tablespoons mixed pickling spices without red pepper pods

1. Wash and put cucumbers in single layers in crock with four layers of leaves between each layer. Heat 1 cup vinegar to lukewarm, add salt and cold water and pour over. Cover with plate and weight down under brine. Leave for 10 days. Drain, wash well in cold water.

2. Heat to boiling point equal parts vinegar and water. Pour over enough to cover and let stand 3 days.

3. Remove cucumbers and cut lengthwise. Pack in hot, sterilized jars. Combine sugar, 1 cup vinegar and spices. Boil 5 minutes. Pour over cucumbers and seal. Process 5 minutes.

4. Let stand for 2 weeks before using. (Makes 2 pints)

Little yellow "Lemon Cucumbers" make tasty pickles. Try our version given below.

Childress Bread and Butter Pickles

8 cups sliced cucumbers ×4
  Salt
2 cups sliced onions
4 green bell peppers (with red on them if possible)
2 cups distilled white vinegar
2 cups sugar
2 teaspoons dry mustard
2 teaspoons turmeric
2 teaspoons celery seed
1 stick cinnamon (broken)

1. Sprinkle cucumber slices with salt and let soak 1 hour. Wash off with cold water and drain.

2. Cut onion slices crosswise and the pepper in about 1½-inch lengths (remove seeds).

3. Combine vinegar, sugar and spices in large kettle and add the cucumbers, onions and peppers. Bring to a boil and cook 3 to 5 minutes or until cucumbers start to look glassy. Pack into hot, sterilized jars. Seal. Process 5 minutes. (Makes 5 to 6 pints)

Lemon Cucumber Sweet Pickles

1 gallon medium lemon cucumbers, thinly sliced
8 small white onions, sliced
1 green bell pepper, cut in narrow strips
1 red bell pepper, cut in narrow strips
½ cup salt
  Cracked ice

Syrup:
5 cups sugar
1½ teaspoons turmeric
½ teaspoon ground cloves
2 tablespoons mustard seed
2 tablespoons celery seed
5 cups white distilled vinegar

1. Combine vegetables with salt, mix well and cover with cracked ice. Let stand 3 hours. Drain.

2. Combine ingredients for syrup, pour over cucumber mixture and bring to boiling point.

3. Pack in hot, sterilized jars and seal. Process 5 minutes. (Makes 6-8 pints)

Cucumber Sauce for Fish

2 medium cucumbers (½ pound)
3 tablespoons white distilled vinegar
1 teaspoon salt
⅛ teaspoon white pepper

1. Pare and grate or chop cucumbers, mix with vinegar and seasonings.

2. Pack into covered container and refrigerate.

Crystal Cucumbers

4 quarts sliced or cubed cucumbers
1 cup salt
1 gallon water
1 tablespoon alum
1 tablespoon ground ginger

Syrup:
3 cups water
1 quart vinegar
6 cups sugar
1 cinnamon stick
1 tablespoon mixed pickling spices
1 tablespoon celery seed

1. Cover cucumbers with brine of salt and water. Let stand 8 days. Drain and discard brine.

2. Place cucumbers and enough water to cover in a kettle with alum. Bring to a boil, remove from heat and let stand 20 minutes. Drain and discard liquid.

3. Add ginger and enough water to cover. Bring to boil, remove from heat and let stand 30 minutes. Discard liquid.

4. Bring to boil the syrup ingredients with spices tied in cheesecloth bag.

5. Add cucumbers and bring to boil.

6. Pack into hot sterilized jars and seal. Process 5 minutes. (Makes 8 pints)

Curry Pickles

24 medium-sized cucumbers (cubed or thinly sliced)
½ cup salt
8 cups water
1 teaspoon curry powder
2 cups distilled white vinegar
2½ cups sugar
¼ cup mustard seed
1 tablespoon celery seed

1. Wash cucumbers; drain. Combine salt and water. Pour over cucumbers. Let stand 5 hours.

2. Drain and rinse thoroughly. Mix remaining ingredients and heat to boiling.

3. Pack cucumbers into hot sterilized jars and pour over hot syrup.

4. Process in boiling water bath for 5 minutes. (Makes 8 pints)

Sour Pickles

Medium-sized cucumbers
1 gallon cider vinegar
1 quart water
1 cup salt
1 cup sugar
1 cup mustard seed

1. Wash cucumbers and pack into hot sterilized jars.

2. Combine remaining ingredients in a large pot and bring to a boil. Pour boiling solution over cucumbers.

3. Seal. Process in boiling water bath for 5 minutes.

Quick Sour Pickles

32 cucumbers, about 4 inches long
1 cup salt
4 quarts water
4 cups distilled white vinegar
1 cup sugar
½ tablespoon whole cloves
½ tablespoon mustard seed
½ tablespoon celery seed
½ tablespoon black peppercorns

1. Wash cucumbers. Place in a clean crock.

2. Dissolve salt in water and pour over. Let stand 24 hours. Drain.

3. Place in cold, fresh water for 20 minutes. Drain and taste. If too salty, repeat this step.

4. Cut cucumbers in half lengthwise or in strips according to their size. Place in a clean crock.

5. Combine vinegar and sugar. Add the spices, tied in a cheesecloth bag. Bring to a boil and boil for 5 minutes.

6. Remove spice bag and pour boiling hot syrup over cucumbers. Let stand 24 hours.

7. Drain off syrup and pack cucumbers in hot, sterilized jars.

8. Heat syrup to a rolling boil and fill the jars. Seal. (Makes 8 pints)

Lazy Day Pickles

6-8 quarts small cucumbers

1. Pack cucumbers into sterilized jars.

2. Mix until dissolved:

1 cup salt
1 cup dry mustard
1 gallon distilled white vinegar

3. Pour over. Cover and seal. Process 5 minutes. Ready in about 4 to 5 weeks.
(Makes about 6 to 8 quarts)

Easy Sweet Pickles

1 gallon commercially packed sliced hamburger dills
5 pounds sugar

1. Drain liquid from dill pickles.

2. Cover with sugar in original jar. Turn jar upside down several times to mix thoroughly and dissolve sugar. Ready to eat in about 24 hours.

3. Pack into hot sterilized jars. Process 5 minutes.

Low Calorie Sweet Spiced Pickles

5 pounds small cucumbers
½ cup salt
5 cups water
2 cups distilled white vinegar
3 to 4 tablespoons artificial sweetener
1 teaspoon cinnamon
¼ teaspoon ground allspice
¼ teaspoon ground cloves

1. Scrub cucumbers, place in bowl with salt and add 3 cups water. Let stand 24 hours.

2. Drain and rinse in cold water, then drop into boiling water and drain.

3. Pack cucumbers in sterilized jars.

4. Combine vinegar with remaining 2 cups water, sweetener and spices. Bring to a rapid boil.

5. Pour over cucumbers to within ½ inch of top. Seal. Process in boiling water bath 10 minutes. (Makes 8-10 pints)

Spicy Diet Pickles

4 quarts small cucumbers
1 teaspoon artificial sweetener
3 tablespoons mixed pickling spice
1 tablespoon alum
1 gallon cider vinegar
3 tablespoons dry mustard
¾ cup salt
3 cloves, garlic, slivered

1. Scrub, dry and pack the cucumbers in sterilized jars.

2. Combine the remaining ingredients, stirring to dissolve the salts.

3. Pour over the pickles and seal jars. Process 10 minutes. (Makes about 8 pints)

Atjar (Fresh Indonesian Pickle)

2 cucumbers
2 small onions, sliced very thin
2 cloves of garlic, finely minced
½ teaspoon salt
½ cup distilled white vinegar
2½ tablespoons sugar
2 red hot peppers, thinly sliced, with seeds removed

A large glass jar makes an attractive pickle crock, allowing you to watch what's happening during the brining process.

1. Peel cucumbers and cut lengthwise. Scoop out the seeds with a spoon. Cut the flesh in thin matchstick strips, about 2½ inches long.

2. Combine the cucumber strips with the other ingredients and refrigerate several hours before serving. (Makes about 1 quart)

Eggplant

A warm-weather crop, eggplants can be gathered in "miniature" or very young stages and pickled whole or made into delicious relishes.

Italian Pickled Tiny Eggplants

2 pounds tiny eggplants
3 cloves garlic, minced
2 teaspoons salt
¾ cup red wine vinegar
1 teaspoon freshly ground black pepper
2 teaspoons chopped fresh basil or
½ teaspoon dried
2 teaspoons chopped fresh oregano or
½ teaspoon dried
¼ cup olive oil

1. Pierce eggplants in several places with skewer or fork. Then parboil in boiling, salted water for 10 minutes. Drain.

2. Mash the minced garlic with the salt in a crock, using a wooden spoon.

3. Add the eggplants, vinegar, pepper and herbs. Gently stir the oil, cover and refrigerate. Toss the mixture lightly once a day.

4. It is ready to eat after 24 hours. It can be stored 1 week under refrigeration. (Makes 2 pints)

Eggplant Caviar

"I know some people who prefer this to the real thing."

1 large eggplant
2 small onions, minced
1 clove garlic, minced
½ teaspoon ground clove
1 large ripe tomato, peeled and minced
2 tablespoons white wine vinegar
5 tablespoons olive oil
Salt and pepper to taste
1 tablespoon minced parsley

1. Bake eggplant in a shallow pan at 375 degrees for 50 minutes, or until soft.

2. Dip in cold water and peel off skin. Dice eggplant into small pieces.

3. Mix the eggplant with remaining ingredients and refrigerate several hours. It keeps for several days refrigerated.

4. Serve on sesame crackers or lahvosh (Armenian crackers) or mound on lettuce leaves and sliced tomatoes. (Makes 4 servings)

Syrian Eggplant Relish "Baba Ghanouj" (recipe above) is a great beginning for a Middle Eastern meal. Eat as a dip with pita bread.

O-Shinko is a Japanese classic. The cold pickled spinach should be served with soy sauce in individual bowls.

Baba Ghanouj
(Syrian Eggplant Relish)

2 eggplants
    Juice of 4 lemons
4 cloves garlic, minced
2 tablespoons tahini (sesame paste)
    Salt to taste
1 tomato, peeled and chopped fine
½ cup chopped parsley
¼ cup chopped pomegranate seed
4 tablespoons olive oil
    Pita bread for serving

1. Place eggplants over charcoal grill or under a broiler and cook whole until soft and all sides are charred. Dip into cold water and let cool.

2. Peel off skin and dice eggplants. Place in bowl, mash, mix in lemon juice, garlic, tahini and salt. Add tomatoes and parsley. Mix well.

3. Cover and chill several hours.

4. Serve in a flat dish and garnish with pomegranate seeds. Sprinkle oil over surface. Dip with pita bread. Refrigerated, it keeps for 2 weeks. (Makes about 3 cups)

Note: If desired stir in a few tablespoons of humus (garbanzo spread, available in Middle Eastern specialty stores.)

Greens

Pickled lettuce, spinach, mustard? Try some of the Far Eastern methods of quick-pickling or make products similar to sauerkraut.

Lettuce "Kraut"

Just like sauerkraut

10 pounds lettuce, iceberg or romaine
¼ pound salt
    Brine (1 quart water and 2 tablespoons salt)

1. Shred lettuce coarsely and mix thoroughly with the salt. Pack tightly in a crock.

2. Cover lettuce with a plate weighted down with a heavy object and let stand for 2 weeks or until pickled.

3. Pack into jars with the liquid and fill the jars with additional brine if necessary. Process 20 minutes. (Makes 2 quarts)

O-Shinko Spinach (Japanese Pickled Leaf Spinach)

1½ cups salt
20 pounds leaf spinach, well cleaned
    Water

1. Sprinkle a little salt on the bottom of a large crock. Place a layer of spinach leaves over the salt and sprinkle lightly with more salt. Continue layering in this way until all spinach is used.

2. Add water to cover the spinach halfway.

3. Cover leaves with a plate and weight down with a very heavy object (at least 20 pounds). Store in a cool place.

4. After several days the plate will be entirely submerged in liquid and the pickle is ready to eat. Serve with soy sauce.

Herbs

Successful pickling is dependent upon herbs. Various blends of herbs and spices create a variety of flavors from a single vegetable or fruit. We offer suggestions for seasonings on pages 94-95.

There is nothing like the taste and aroma of fresh herbs. Grow some indoors or out. Or learn good sources of fresh ones grown in your area. If you must resort to dried products, make sure they are fresh. They do not last forever and your herb shelves should be restocked when potency is lost.

In addition to using herbs as flavor accents, here is a method of preserving herbs by a simple pickling process.

And don't forget the beautifully flavored herb vinegars as shown on page 77.

Pickled Herbs

Sprigs of fresh herbs (tarragon, basil, dill weed, oregano, etc.)
White wine vinegar

1. Wash fresh herbs quickly and pat dry with paper towels. Pack sprigs (or leaves) into hot, sterilized jars.

2. Heat white wine vinegar just to boiling and slowly pour over herbs, filling the bottle. Seal. Use in cooking anywhere herbs are called for; or toss in salads, mix in dressings, or use as garnishes.

Horseradish

Three to four plants will supply the average family with plenty of hot, zesty relish. Harvest in fall. Store roots in cool place and make fresh batches of products frequently. Keep them stored in refrigerator. Look for fresh roots in the produce section of your market.

Horseradish Relish

2 fresh horseradish roots (approximately)
½ cup distilled white vinegar
¼ teaspoon salt
    Sugar (to taste, if desired)

1. Wash roots and peel away brown skin.

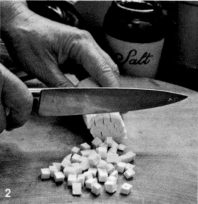

Horseradish relish should be made in small quantities to insure full potency and hot taste. **1.** *Peel washed roots with a vegetable peeler.* **2.** *Cut into small cubes with a sharp knife.* **3.** *Place horseradish in a blender with vinegar, salt and sugar. Grate to desired consistency. (This can also be done with a grater.)* **4.** *Pour into small jars and store in the refrigerator.*

2. Grate root. Or cube and put through food chopper or blender with vinegar and salt. Measure. You need 1 cup grated horseradish.

3. Pack in jar. Seal tightly. Store in refrigerator. (Make 1 cup)

Horseradish Relish

3 quarts peeled, chopped tomatoes
¾ cup freshly grated horseradish
1 hot red pepper, seeded and chopped
1 cup chopped celery
1 cup chopped onion
¾ cup light brown sugar
1½ cups cider vinegar
2 tablespoons salt
1 teaspoon ground allspice
½ teaspoon cinnamon
½ teaspoon ground cloves
3 tablespoons mustard seed
1 tablespoon dill seed

1. Using a colander, drain juice from tomatoes. (Use it for soup or beverage)

2. Put the tomatoes, horseradish, pepper, celery and onions in a large kettle.

3. In another pot, bring the remaining ingredients to a boil. Pour the boiling liquid over the vegetables and simmer the mixture until thickened.

4. Spoon relish into hot sterilized jars and seal. (Makes 4 to 5 pints)

Saucy Cinnamon Relish

2 cups applesauce
½ cup diced celery
½ cup seedless raisins
½ cup red cinnamon candies
½ cup prepared horseradish

1. Combine ingredients and chill in refrigerator several hours.

2. Before serving, stir until candies are completely dissolved and mixed through applesauce. Serve with pork roast or baked ham. (Makes about 3½ cups)

Jerusalem artichokes

Another versatile root crop that makes a delicious crunchy pickled product. Peel away the brown skin before using.

Jerusalem Artichoke Mustard Pickles

10 pounds small Jerusalem artichokes
2 large onions, sliced
2 cups sugar
¼ pound mustard
4 tablespoons turmeric
4 tablespoons mixed pickling spice
1 cup salt
3 quarts distilled white vinegar

1. Scrub artichokes, rinse and drain. Pack in jars with sliced onions.

2. Mix the dry ingredients with a little of the vinegar until smooth.

3. Gradually add the rest of the vinegar, bring to a boil and pour over artichokes.

4. Seal and process in boiling water bath for 15 minutes. (Makes 4 quarts)

Pickled Jerusalem Artichokes

1 gallon Jerusalem artichokes
1½ cups sugar
1 clove garlic
1 tablespoon turmeric
3 tablespoons mixed pickling spice
3 quarts distilled white vinegar
3 tablespoons salt

1. Scrub artichokes, rinse and drain. Pack into hot jars.

2. Combine remaining ingredients, bring to a boil and simmer 15 minutes. Pour over artichokes.

3. Seal and process in boiling water bath for 15 minutes. (Makes 4 quarts)

Artichoke Relish

1 peck Jerusalem artichokes, well scrubbed
Brine: 2 cups salt to 1 gallon water
2 quarts onions
2 cups celery
8 green bell peppers
1 tablespoon diced pimento or red pepper
¼ cup dry mustard
8 tablespoons turmeric
2 cups all-purpose flour
3 cups water
3¾ quarts vinegar
4 cups sugar
1 tablespoon black pepper

1. Soak artichokes in brine overnight. Drain. Grind artichokes, onions, celery and green bell peppers. Add pimento or red pepper. Place in kettle.

2. Mix together mustard, turmeric, flour and enough water to make a paste. Stir into the kettle and add vinegar, remaining water, sugar and black pepper. Cook, stirring constantly, until thickened.

3. Pack into hot, sterilized jars. Seal. Process 15 minutes.

Mushrooms

Play it safe and get your fresh mushrooms from commercial sources. These strange creatures have little nutritive value, but do miracles for the taste buds. Dried mushrooms do not pickle successfully.

Pickled Mushrooms in Wine Vinegar

½ cup lemon juice or 1¼ teaspoons granular citric acid
1 quart water
6 cups small button mushrooms, washed

2 tablespoons mixed pickling spices or
  1 teaspoon *each* oregano and basil,
  6 bay leaves and 2 cloves garlic
1 quart distilled white vinegar

1. Combine lemon juice or citric acid with water in a large saucepan.

2. Add mushrooms and bring to boil. Simmer for 5 minutes.

3. Drain and place in sterilized half-pint jars.

4. Tie pickling spices and herbs in a cheesecloth bag and place in a saucepan with vinegar. Bring to a boil and simmer 1 minute.

5. Pour over mushrooms in jars, leaving ¼ inch headspace. Seal jars and process in boiling water bath for 20 minutes. (Makes 6 half-pints)

Middle-Eastern Mushrooms

4 pounds small mushrooms, washed
1 tablespoon salt
Juice of 2 lemons
Water
1 quart distilled vinegar
1 cup olive oil
1½ teaspoon powdered thyme
1 tablespoon freshly ground pepper

1. Clean mushrooms. Place in a saucepan with salt, lemon juice and enough water just to cover. Cover and simmer 6 minutes. Drain.

2. Combine vinegar, oil, thyme and pepper in pot and heat to boiling.

3. Pack mushrooms in sterilized pint jars. Pour hot vinegar mixture over mushrooms. Seal. Process 20 minutes. (Makes 4 pints)

Pickled Mushrooms in Oil

½ cup lemon juice or 1¼ teaspoon citric acid
1 quart water
6 cups small button mushrooms, washed
1 teaspoon salt
2 cups distilled white vinegar
½ teaspoon each dried oregano and basil
2 bay leaves, broken in half
2 cloves garlic
½ cup olive oil and 1 cup salad oil or 1½ cups olive oil

1. Combine lemon juice or citric acid and water in a large saucepan.

2. Add mushrooms and salt and bring to a boil. Simmer 5 minutes.

3. Drain and pour vinegar over. Cover and let stand 10 to 12 hours.

4. Drain mushrooms and reserve vinegar (vinegar can be used one more time in pickling mushrooms or use in salad dressings or cooking.) Place mushrooms in sterilized half-pint jars.

5. Divide herbs into 4 portions and add to jars. Cover with olive oil or a mixture of olive oil and salad oil.

6. Process in a boiling water bath 20 minutes. (Makes 4 half-pints)

"Dill Pickled Okra" (recipe below) is a spicy hot taste treat perfect for a backyard barbecue or with drinks.

Pickled Mushroom Buttons

2 pounds small, button mushrooms, washed
1 small onion, peeled and chopped
2 teaspoons salt
6 black peppercorns
2 teaspoons ground ginger
1 teaspoon ground mace
  Distilled white vinegar to fill jars

1. Place mushrooms, onion, salt, peppercorns, ginger and mace in a pan and add vinegar to cover. Bring to a boil, cover and simmer until mushrooms are barely tender, about 3 to 5 minutes.

2. Pack mushrooms into hot, sterilized jars. Strain vinegar, bring to boil and pour into jars. Seal. Process 20 minutes. (Makes 3 pints)

Okra

Usually thought of in relationship to the southern states for gardeners, the pods are available throughout the country in greengrocers. They make one of the finest pickles.

Sweet & Sour Okra Pickle

Mature okra can be used in this version.

3 pounds okra
1 pound small white onions, peeled
2 sweet red bell peppers
3 cups cider vinegar
1 cup water
1 teaspoon salt
1¾ cup sugar
1 tablespoon mustard seed
2 cloves garlic, slivered
1 teaspoon whole cloves
1 teaspoon whole allspice

1. Parboil the okra and onions just until they begin to get tender. Rinse immediately in cold water. Cut the okra in 1-inch pieces and grate onions lengthwise.

2. Seed the peppers and cut in 1-inch pieces. Combine the vegetables and pack into sterilized jars.

3. Bring the remaining ingredients to a boil and simmer 10 minutes. Pour over the vegetables. Seal. Process 5 minutes. (Makes 4 pints)

Dill Pickled Okra

2 pounds young okra
  Celery leaves
4 cloves garlic
4 sprigs dill
2 cups water
2 cups distilled white vinegar
2 tablespoons salt

1. Scrub okra and pack whole pods into sterilized jars.

2. In each jar insert a few celery leaves, 1 garlic clove, peeled and 1 sprig of dill.

3. Bring water, vinegar and salt to a boil.

4. Pour the boiling liquid over the okra and seal jars. Process 5 minutes. Let the okra stand for about 1 month before using. (Makes 4 pints)

Hot Pickled Okra

6 pounds young okra
1 quart distilled white vinegar
1 quart water
½ cup salt
4 hot red pepper pods, minced seeds removed
2 cloves garlic, minced
1 tablespoon szichwan or java pepper, crushed
1 tablespoon mustard seed

1. Wash okra and pack into hot, sterilized jars.

2. Boil the remaining ingredients together for 10 minutes and pour over okra. Seal. Process 5 minutes. (Makes 10 pints)

Louisiana Pickled Okra

2 pounds fresh young okra pods
10 cloves garlic, peeled
5 hot red peppers
4 cups distilled white vinegar
1 cup water
6 tablespoons salt
2 bay leaves
1 tablespoon celery seeds
1 teaspoon white peppercorns

1. Wash okra and pack it into sterilized half-pint jars. Put two garlic cloves and 1 red pepper in each jar.

2. Bring the remaining ingredients to a boil and pour over the okra. Seal. Process 5 minutes.

3. Let stand at least 1 month before using. (Makes 5 half-pints)

Olives

Fresh olives are available in the California area. Those who live cross-country may be able to have some shipped from friends or relatives at harvest time.

Preparation is difficult and time-consuming. However, we feel that the curing process is interesting and challenging to the adventurous pickler.

Home cured olives should be used soon after completing. Canning is not recommended.

Should you desire to know more about home processing of olives order bulletin Number HXT-29 from University of California Cooperative Extension Service, 90 University Hall, Berkeley, CA 94720.

Ripe Olives

This thorough process comes from the College of Agriculture, University of California.

1. *THE FRUIT:* Use firm, freshly-picked olives ranging from the straw-yellow to light-pink stage of maturity. Black olives are too ripe and will usually give a soft pickled product. The 'Mission' and 'Manzanillo' varieties are best for the beginner.

2. *CONTAINER:* To hold the olives during pickling, use a stoneware crock or a wooden tub. A barrel cut in half makes two suitable pickling tubs. Never use a zinc bucket or other metal container.

3. *FIRST LYE:* Prepare a lye solution containing 2 ounces of ordinary flake or granular lye (caustic soda) to each gallon of water. A convenient method of preparing the solution is to note the contents of the can (usually 12 ounces) and add the contents to the required amount of water. When the lye is well dissolved in the required amount of water, add enough to the olives to cover them well.

CAUTION: Lye is corrosive to skin and clothes. Have at hand a cup of vinegar and rinse hands in it to neutralize any lye present on the skin, any lye solution that may get on the clothes.

Stir once an hour and occasionally cut several olives with a knife and note the penetration of lye; as the lye enters the olive the flesh is turned to a yellowish color. Allow the lye to remain until the skins of all the olives are well penetrated, and the lye has entered the flesh to a depth of about 1/32 inch or less. The time required varies with the temperature, the variety and the lye concentration. Usually 4 to 5 hours is required. The purpose of the first lye is to facilitate the darkening of the olives; if the lye penetrates too deeply the color will fail to darken properly.

When the desired penetration has been attained, remove and discard the lye solution.

4. *DARKENING OF COLOR:* Rinse the olives with water; discard the water and leave the olives exposed to the air to darken. Twice a day for 4 days cover the olives with water, stir, discard the water and leave exposed to air.

5. *SECOND LYE:* Prepare a new lye solution of 1 ounce of lye per gallon. Cover the olives with it and allow to penetrate about halfway to the pit. This will require about 3 to 4 hours.

Remove the lye and discard it. This lye is also to facilitate the darkening.

6. *SECOND EXPOSURE:* Rinse once in water and expose to the air for 24 hours, stirring occasionally during this exposure.

7. *THIRD LYE:* Prepare another lye solution of 1 ounce of lye per gallon. Place on the olives and allow to penetrate to the pit—about 4 to 6 hours is usually required. The purpose of this lye is to destroy the natural olive bitterness and must be allowed to completely reach the pit. This is judged by cutting several olives with a knife and noting depth of penetration. If the lye fails to reach the pits in 15 hours, prepare and apply a fresh lye of ¾ ounce of lye per gallon until it reaches the pits.

8. *THIRD EXPOSURE:* Rinse olives in water and expose 24 hours to darken the color still further.

9. *WASHING:* Cover olives with water. Change the water twice a day for a week. The olives should now be free of the taste of lye. Absence of lye or its presence in the olives is easily detected by taste; the amount present is harmless to the taster.

10. *BRINING:* Prepare a brine of about ¼ pound of salt per gallon (that is, 4 ounces per gallon or 1 pound to 4 gallons of water). Cover the olives with this brine for 2 days. They are then ready to serve.

11. *STORAGE:* To keep the olives for several weeks replace this brine after 1 week with a fresh brine of 8 ounces salt to 1 gallon water. Store in this brine 1 week. Replace it with a fresh brine of 12 ounces salt to 1 gallon water. Change this brine once every 3 weeks until the olives are consumed, each time preparing a fresh brine of 3 pounds salt to 4 gallons water.

The olives will shrivel somewhat in this brine and are too salty to eat. Therefore, soak them in water overnight before serving. A weaker brine than the above is extremely dangerous, even if the olives are stored in open containers. Take no chances —use the brine as directed.

Green Olives, Spanish Style

1. Select green full size olives; 'Sevillano' and 'Manzanillo' varieties.

2. Dissolve 2½ ounces of lye to 1 gallon water and stir well. Cover olives with lye solution in a crock or wooden tub. Allow to stand until lye has penetrated ⅔ of the way to the pit. Check by cutting frequently. It usually takes 5 to 7 hours.

3. Discard lye and plunge olives into cold water. Pour off and replace with fresh, cold water. Repeat this at least 4 times per day for 2 days.

4. Pour olives in a barrel or keg. Fill with brine containing:

   1 pound salt to each:
   1 gallon of water

To each 5 gallon keg add:

½ pint vinegar
1 pint Spanish olive brine or sour dill pickle brine
½ pint light corn syrup

Mix olives and brine well.

5. Seal container, leaving ¼-inch opening to allow escape of gas. When gas evolution ceases, seal the opening. The barrel must be filled with brine at all times. (10 ounces salt to 1 gallon water). Store in a warm place for about 6 months.

6. When barrel is opened, add to each 5 gallons olives about 1 quart distilled, white vinegar. Pour into glass jars with glass tops. (Do not use zinc-tops). Seal. It is not necessary to treat further. Keep refrigerated.

Greek Olives

Black ripe olives ('Mission' or 'Manzanillo')
Rock salt
Coarse salt
Olive oil

1. Line shallow wooden boxes with burlap. Mix 5 pounds salt with each 10 pounds olives and spread in box.

2. Stir well once a week. An easy way is to pour from one box to another, allowing brine to seep away.

3. Olives should be ready in 6 weeks. They will have lost bitterness and be somewhat shriveled. Turn into a bowl and add some coarse salt and a little olive oil. Stir to coat. Pack into jars and refrigerate. Eat before completely dried. To serve, drizzle with a little olive oil, sprinkle with crumbled oregano and squeeze a little lemon juice over olives.

Mock Olives

4 pounds green plums (small, immature purple plums)
Brine:
½ cup salt to 3 quarts water
1 teaspoon baking soda

1. Soak plums in brine 24 hours.

2. Drain plums and place in a fresh batch of brine with the soda. Bring to boil. Cook until plums turn olive green in color.

3. Pack in hot, sterilized jars. Seal. Process 20 minutes. (Makes 4 pints)

Olives are soaked with lye solution several times, thoroughly rinsed and cut to check color change caused by lye penetration.

A sunny Mediterranean picnic features "Grape Leaves" (page 73) which have been stuffed and "Greek Olives" (page 46).

Onions

Most onions used in pickling are sun-dried prior to storing. If you purchase them from a market this job has been completed for you. They are an invaluable part of many pickled products. Here are some ways of placing the onion in the spotlight.

Pickled Cocktail Onions

4 quarts tiny white onions
1 cup salt
2 quarts distilled white vinegar
2 cups sugar
3 tablespoons mustard seed
3 tablespoons whole black pepper
3 tablespoons grated horseradish
Small red peppers
Bay leaves

1. Cover onions with boiling water. Let stand 2 minutes. Drain and cover with cold water. Peel.

2. Sprinkle with salt and cover with water. Let stand overnight.

3. In the morning, drain. Wash well with cold water and drain again.

4. Combine vinegar, sugar, mustard seed, black pepper and horseradish in large kettle. Boil 2 minutes.

5. Add onions and bring to boil again.

6. Pack onions into hot, sterilized jars. Add a pepper and a bay leaf to each jar. Fill with boiling syrup and seal. Process 5 minutes.
(Makes 6 pints)

Sweet Onion Relish

12 large sweet onions
(about 4 pounds), peeled
1 tablespoon salt
2 green apples
2 red bell peppers
1 cup cider vinegar
1 cup sugar
1 tablespoon fresh tarragon
(¾ teaspoon dried)
1 teaspoon white pepper
1 teaspoon ground mace

1. Put onions through medium blade of food chopper, mix them with the salt and let stand overnight.

2. Press out most of the onion juice through a strainer. (Save for soup.)

3. Core apples and seed peppers. Chop them finely.

4. Combine all ingredients in a heavy pot and bring to a gentle boil. Simmer 10 minutes.

5. Turn into hot, sterilized jars. Seal. Process 5 minutes. (Makes 3 pints)

Oriental vegetable pickles include (top to bottom) Kim Chee, Daikon, Water Chestnuts, Snow Peas, and Mustard Cabbage.

Oriental vegetables

Pickles originated in the orient. Today they are still served with every Japanese meal and comprise an important part of Chinese and other Far Eastern cuisine. Methods vary from Western pickling in that salt plays a more important role and the process is much quicker.

Oriental vegetables—Daikon; Cabbages Wong Bok, Pak Choy, Kai Choy; Bitter melons; Ginger root; Mung beans to name but a few. Try "Western" vegetables pickled in the "Oriental" manner.

Pickled Daikon and Carrot

½ pound daikon (white radish)
peeled and shredded
1 carrot shredded
1 tablespoon salt
1 cup water
1 tablespoon distilled white vinegar
1 teaspoon sugar

1. Put vegetables, salt and water into a bowl and let stand 30 minutes.

2. Drain off water and squeeze vegetables as dry as possible.

3. Combine vegetables with vinegar and sugar in a bowl.

4. Serve at room temperature. (Makes 6 servings)

Singari Daikon

4 ounces dried daikon (white radish)
1 cup carrots, cut into thin strips
1 tablespoon minced fresh ginger
2 tablespoons soy sauce
1 small piece dashi knobu
(seaweed flavoring, available at Oriental markets)
3 tablespoons cider vinegar
1 tablespoon sugar

1. Combine all ingredients in a bowl. Cover mixture with a plate weighted with a heavy object. Leave at room temperature about 5 days or until liquid rises to the top.

2. Refrigerate 7 days.

3. Serve as a side dish with plain boiled rice. (Makes 1½ cups)

O-Shinko (Japanese pickled greens)

Greens of turnips, lettuce, collards, beets, dandelions, chard or Chinese cabbage can be pickled in the same manner as O-Shinko Spinach on page 43.

Kim Chee (Korean Pickled Cabbage)

2 pounds Chinese cabbage
½ cup coarse salt
4 cups water
1½ tablespoons minced hot red pepper
2 cloves garlic, finely minced
1½ teaspoons minced fresh ginger root
1 tablespoon sugar
2 scallions, chopped

1. Cut cabbage in 1½ inch squares. Put in a bowl with salt and water and let stand overnight.

2. Drain, then rinse in cold water and drain again.

3. Combine remaining ingredients with cabbage, mixing well.

4. Pack into a quart jar and refrigerate 4 to 5 days before serving. (Makes 1 quart)

Chinese Cabbage Pickle

3 pounds bok choy or Wong Bok
(Chinese cabbages) or
Pak Choy (Chinese mustard cabbage)
3 tablespoons salt
1 hot pepper, sliced
1 strip dashi knobu (seaweed flavoring)

1. Cut cabbage lengthwise into strips. In a large crock build up layers of cabbage and salt with the pepper added at equal intervals. The cabbage strip layers should alternate direction.

2. Break dashi knobu into three strips and force them down through the layers of cabbage.

3. Weight down cabbage with a cover and heavy object. Let the crock stand for about 3 days at room temperature, or until the vegetable is submerged in water.

4. To serve, rinse off strips and cut into 1-inch slices. Dip in soy sauce. (Makes 1 quart)

Pickled Chinese Snow Pea

4 pounds sugar pea pods
2 quarts distilled white vinegar
¼ cup salt
½ cup sugar
2 cups water
3 tablespoons mixed pickling spice

1. Wash pea pods, remove ends and string. Steam for 5 minutes over boiling water. Immediately rinse under cold water.

2. Combine remaining ingredients in a pot and bring to a boil. Simmer 10 minutes.

3. Pack pea pods in hot, sterilized jars. Pour strained hot vinegar mixture over them. Seal. Process 5 minutes. (Makes 4 quarts)

Pickled Water Chestnut

5 pounds peeled water chestnuts
2 inch section ginger root, sliced
very thinly
1 cup sugar
3 tablespoons mustard seed
6 hot red peppers, sliced in small rings
(seeds removed)
½ cup salt
6 cups distilled white vinegar

1. Cook chestnuts in boiling, salted water 10 minutes. Drain and pack into hot, sterilized jars.

2. Combine remaining ingredients and bring to boil. Simmer 10 minutes.

3. Pour vinegar mixture over chestnuts. Seal: Process 10 minutes. (Makes 2 quarts)

Sweet and Sour Sauce

1 cup pineapple juice
¼ cup peanut oil
2 tablespoons sesame oil
4 teaspoons brown sugar
2 teaspoons soy sauce
1 teaspoon cayenne
½ cup rice wine vinegar
1 tablespoon cornstarch mixed with
  2 tablespoons water

1. Combine all ingredients, except cornstarch and water, in a pot. Bring to boil.

2. Add cornstarch mixture, stirring constantly. Simmer until sauce is thickened and transparent. Store in a covered jar in the refrigerator. (Makes 1 pint)

Peppers

Maybe you can't follow Peter Piper's trend of picking pre-pickled peppers, but you can easily pickle your own. And the possibilities range from delicate, sweet flavors to hot, tearful relishes.

Size is a good indicator of hotness. Usually the smaller the hot varieties, the hotter the pepper. Sweet peppers can be harvested and pickled green or left to mature to red, a beautiful pickling possibility.

Pickled Peppers

4 quarts long red, green or
  yellow peppers
1½ cups salt
2 cloves garlic
2 tablespoons prepared horseradish
10 cups distilled white vinegar
2 cups water
¼ cup sugar

1. Cut two small slits in each pepper. (Wear rubber gloves to prevent burning hands. Keep hands away from eyes to avoid irritation.)

2. Dissolve salt in 4 quarts water. Pour over peppers and let stand 12 to 18 hours in a cool place. Drain, rinse and drain thoroughly.

3. Combine remaining ingredients; simmer 15 minutes. Remove garlic.

4. Pack peppers into hot, sterilized jars. Seal. Process pints 10 minutes in boiling water bath (Makes 8 pints)

Pickled Stuffed Peppers

12 green peppers
1 cup plus 1 tablespoon salt
1 gallon water
1½ quarts shredded cabbage
1 cup chopped onion

1 cup minced celery
3 cloves garlic, minced
2 tablespoons mustard seed
3 tablespoons celery seed
½ cup sugar
1 quart tarragon-flavored white wine
  vinegar

1. Remove stems and seeds from the peppers, leaving shells whole. Place peppers with 1 cup salt and water in a crock. Weight down and let stand overnight.

2. Salt cabbage with the remaining salt. Let stand while preparing remaining ingredients. Combine onions, celery, garlic, seeds and sugar with drained cabbage.

3. Rinse peppers and stuff them with cabbage mixture. Pack them into sterilized jars and fill with boiling vinegar. Seal. Process 10 minutes.

4. This pickle takes 4 weeks to mature. (Makes 3 pints)

Pickled Peppers

Sweet red or green peppers or fresh
  pimientos, stemmed and seeded,
  then cut in thirds
Water
Distilled white vinegar
½ teaspoon salt per quart
1 teaspoon sugar per quart

1. Bring equal parts vinegar and water to a boil (enough to fill jars).

2. Drop peppers into boiling liquid. Simmer 5 minutes.

3. Pack into hot, sterilized jars. Add salt and sugar. Fill with hot liquid.

4. Seal. Process 5 minutes.

Pepper Hash

12 sweet red peppers, seeded
12 sweet green peppers, seeded
2 medium-sized onions
1 quart boiling water
2 cups cider vinegar
2 cups sugar
½ teaspoon salt

1. Put vegetables through the coarse blade of a food chopper. Cover with boiling water and let stand 10 minutes.

2. Drain off water, pouring through a strainer or cloth bag.

3. Combine vinegar, sugar and salt with vegetables in a kettle. Bring to a boil and simmer 20 minutes.

4. Pour into hot, sterilized jars and seal. Process 5 minutes. (Makes 4 pints)

Marge's Three or Four Pepper Salsa

"This is for those who have a surplus of peppers in their garden. Good with meat, eggs, or crackers and a slice of cheese."

3 sweet banana peppers
3 Hungarian wax peppers

2 Anaheim peppers (long green sweet)
2 Jalapeño peppers
2 pounds tomatoes
4 tomatillos
1 large onion, peeled
3 cloves garlic, peeled
2 shallots (optional), peeled
1 teaspoon salt
  Olive oil
  Small handful cilantro (optional)

1. Stem and seed all peppers. Blend all ingredients in a blender.

2. Cook in a small amount of oil for 15 minutes, or until glazed and tender. Serve hot or cold. Salsa can be frozen or stored in the refrigerator.

Note: Vary the amount of hot peppers to suit your own taste. If you have a very hot green chile and want to take some of the heat out, remove seeds, stems and veins and soak in cold, salted water or a brine made of 1 tablespoon vinegar to 2 cups water for an hour or longer. It is a good idea to wear rubber gloves when cutting hot chilies.

Salsa de Chile Guero
(Green Chile Sauce)

Excellent with fish, chicken, eggs, and cheese.

4 sweet long green chilies
1 large tomato, peeled, seeded and
  chopped or about 1 pound fresh
  tomatillos
6 sprigs parsley, chopped or cilantro
1 small white onion, chopped
1 clove garlic
1 serrano chile
  Salt, pepper, pinch of sugar
3 tablespoons salad oil

1. Simmer the fresh chilies in boiling water for 5 minutes. Drain, remove seeds and stems.

2. Put all ingredients in blender and blend for 2 or 3 seconds.

3. Heat oil in a large frying pan and cook mixture about 5 minutes, or until glazed. (Makes about 1½ cups)

Jalapeño Sauce

1 pound Jalapeño peppers (fresh and
  firm)
1 pound onions (4 medium),
  peeled and chopped
1 pound peeled fresh tomatoes
  (1 quart)
1 teaspoon salt
½ cup distilled white vinegar
1 teaspoon garlic salt

1. Cut stems and remove seed from peppers, wash and place in pot with onions and tomatoes.

2. Add remaining ingredients and cook about 1 hour, or until onions are soft.

3. Purée in a blender and store in the refrigerator. (Makes about 3 pints)

Note: Wear gloves when removing seeds from peppers.

Bowls of Pickled Hot Peppers (below), Jalapeño Sauce (page 50) and Salsa de Chile Guero (page 50) are guaranteed to add spice to any Mexican dinner.

Creole Hot Sauce

72 hot red peppers
2 cloves garlic, minced
2 cups water
2 tablespoons sugar
1 teaspoon salt
4 teaspoons grated horseradish
2 cups distilled white vinegar

1. Wash peppers and combine with garlic.

2. Place in saucepan with water. Cover and cook until very tender.

3. Press through sieve.

4. Add remaining ingredients. Cook until thickened. Pour into sterilized jars. Seal. Process in boiling water bath for 10 minutes. (Makes about 4 half-pints)

Bell Peppers in Vinegar

4 quarts green bell peppers (cut in quarters or eighths)
4½ quarts distilled white vinegar

1. Wash peppers. Remove core, seeds and stems. Cut as desired, or leave whole after coring. Pack into hot, sterilized jars.

2. Heat vinegar to 150 to 160 degrees. Pour hot vinegar over peppers, covering well. Let stand loosely sealed several days.

3. Pour off the vinegar and replace with fresh vinegar that has been brought to a boil. Add salt to taste.

4. If oil is desired, add fresh vinegar to within ¾ to ⅞ inch of jar top. Add olive oil to the top. The peppers will be coated with oil as they pass through the oil layer with use.

5. Seal and process 5 minutes. (Makes 8 pints)

Pickled Hot Peppers

4 quarts hot peppers
4½ quarts distilled white vinegar

1. Wash peppers thoroughly.

51

Remove core, seeds, and stems of large peppers. Cut as desired, or leave whole after coring. The small, hot peppers may be left whole with stems intact.

2. Heat vinegar to 150 to 160 degrees. (This is about the simmering point.) The vinegar should *not* be allowed to boil.

3. Pack peppers rather tightly into jars. Pour hot vinegar over the peppers.

4. Let stand loosely sealed until bubbling stops. There will be bubbles of gas escaping (gassing) because of microbial and enzymatic activity. This gassing will occur for several days and perhaps as long as 2 weeks. The jars of peppers should not be kept in a hot room and should be watched for signs of spoilage. If the room temperature is below 55 to 60 degrees, proper gassing will not take place.

5. When bubbling stops, pour off vinegar and cover to the top of the jar with fresh vinegar. Add salt to taste, if desired.

6. If oil is desired, add fresh vinegar to within ¾ to ⅞ inch of jar top. Then fill to the top with olive oil. The peppers will be coated with oil as they pass through the oil layer with use.

7. Seal. Process 5 minutes. (Makes 8 pints)

Bell Pepper Relish

12 green bell peppers
12 red bell peppers
12 medium-sized onions
2 cups cider vinegar
2 cups sugar
3 tablespoons salt

1. Remove cores and seeds from peppers and chop finely. Peel onions and chop finely. Cover with boiling water and let stand 5 minutes.

2. Drain and add the vinegar, sugar and salt.

3. Pour into hot, sterilized jars and seal. Process 5 minutes. (Makes 6 pints)

Red Pepper Relish

2 dozen red bell peppers
7 medium-sized onions
2 tablespoons mustard seed
2 tablespoons salt
3 cups distilled white vinegar
3 cups sugar

1. Remove cores and seeds from peppers. Grind peppers and onions, saving the juice.

2. Combine all ingredients. Boil 30 minutes.

3. Pack into sterilized jars. Seal and process in boiling water bath 5 minutes. (Makes 4 pints)

Salted Peppers

Preserved peppers for later use in pickling or stuffing.

Peppers, hot or sweet, red or green
Salt
Water

1. Wash peppers, remove stems, seeds and ribs. Place in container, stem end up.

2. Cover with brine. (Begin with 2 pounds salt to 1 gallon water; add additional salt until no more dissolves.) Weight down or pack in jars and seal. Process 5 minutes.

3. Freshen before using by soaking in cold water.

Radishes

Pickled radishes add a great crunch and pungent flavor to any meal. Easy to grow and economical to buy, they are good alone or mixed with other vegetables.

Red Radish Relish

4 cups red radishes, trimmed to remove tips and stems
3 large stalks celery
2 medium-sized red onions
2½ teaspoons salt
1 cup sugar
1 tablespoon mustard seed
2 teaspoons dill seed
1 teaspoon celery seed
1 cup cider vinegar
2 tablespoons ground horseradish

1. Put the radishes, celery and onion through the coarse blade of the food chopper.

2. Mix the vegetables with the other ingredients and let stand 3 hours.

3. In a large pot bring the mixture to a boil and simmer 10 minutes.

4. Turn immediately into hot, sterilized jars. Seal. Process 20 minutes. (Makes 2 pints)

Radish Pickles

2 quarts radishes, washed, stems and tips removed
½ cup salt
1 quart cold water
4 cups distilled white vinegar
3 tablespoons mixed pickling spices
1 cup sugar

1. Cover radishes with scalding water. Let stand about 3 minutes. Then plunge into solution of salt and cold water. Let stand overnight. Drain.

2. Rinse with cold water; drain again.

3. Mix vinegar, pickling spices and sugar and simmer for 10 minutes.

4. Place radishes into hot, sterilized jars. Bring vinegar mixture to a quick boil. Pour over radishes. Seal. Process 20 minutes. (Makes 4 pints)

Chopping fresh rhubarb for tangy relish.

Rhubarb

This fruit-like vegetable is harvested its second year of growth. Only the stalks are edible which blend beautifully with other flavors. See Chutney on page 62.

Rhubarb Relish

3 quarts chopped rhubarb
5 cups brown sugar, packed
1 cup cider vinegar
3 cups chopped onion
1 tablespoon salt
Spice bag:
3 sticks cinnamon
2 tablespoons mixed pickling spices
4 whole nutmegs
1 tablespoon freshly grated ginger root

1. Mix all ingredients in a large kettle. Bring to a boil and simmer until rhubarb is just tender, about 10 to 15 minutes. Remove spice bag.

2. Pack into hot, sterilized jars. Seal. Process 15 minutes. (Makes 4 pints)

Squash and pumpkins

Zucchini squash is the present rage in pickling. Indeed it does make a delicious, zesty product. Try adapting some of the zucchini recipes around to other summer squash for taste variety.

Pumpkin and winter squash can provide the pickler with a new experience and a delicious culinary treat.

Zucchini Bread and Butter Pickles

1 quart distilled white vinegar
2 cups sugar
3 tablespoons salt
2 teaspoons celery seed
2 teaspoons turmeric or dill seed
1 teaspoon dry mustard
4 quarts sliced zucchini
1 quart sliced onions

1. Bring vinegar, sugar, salt and spices to a boil.

2. Pour over freshly sliced vegetables and let stand 1 hour.

3. Bring to a boil and cook for 3 minutes.

4. Pack into hot, sterilized jars. Seal. Process 10 minutes. (Makes 6 to 7 pints)

Pickled Zucchini

8 onions, thinly sliced
1 gallon zucchini, cut into
** ½-inch slices**
3 green peppers, finely chopped
** (seeds removed)**
½ cup salt
5 cups cider vinegar
5 cups sugar
1½ teaspoons turmeric
2 tablespoons mustard seeds
2 teaspoons celery seeds
1 cinnamon stick, broken into
** 4 pieces**

1. In a large crock, layer the vegetables and salt. Weight it down and let stand in refrigerator 6 hours.

2. Drain vegetables, rinse them and drain again.

3. Put the remaining ingredients in a large kettle and bring to a boil. Simmer for 10 minutes, then add the vegetables and remove from heat immediately.

4. Turn into hot, sterilized jars and seal. Process 5 minutes. (Makes 8 pints)

Zucchini Relish I

10 cups zucchini, ground with skin
4 cups onions, ground
2 cups celery, ground
2 large green bell peppers, ground
5 tablespoons salt
1 tablespoon cornstarch
2½ cups distilled white vinegar
6 cups sugar
1 tablespoon nutmeg
1 tablespoon turmeric
½ tablespoon pepper
** Dash of Tabasco**

1. Mix the vegetables in a large kettle. Add salt and enough cold water to cover. Let stand overnight.

2. Drain liquid and rinse 3 or 4 times.

3. Dissolve cornstarch in a small amount of vinegar. Add remaining vinegar and other ingredients to vegetables.

4. Cover and simmer about 30 minutes or until tender. Pack into hot, sterilized jars. Seal. Process 5 minutes. (Makes 8 pints)

Zucchini Relish II

4 cups ground zucchini
3 cups ground carrot
4½ cups ground onion
1½ cups ground green pepper
¼ cup salt
2¼ cups distilled white vinegar
¾ cup sugar
1 tablespoon celery seed

1. Combine all ingredients in a large kettle.

2. Cover and simmer 20 minutes, or until vegetables are crisp tender.

3. Pack into hot, sterilized jars. Seal. Process in boiling water bath 5 minutes. (Makes 4 to 5 pints)

Latvian Pumpkin Pickle

2 cups water
1 cup sugar
½ cup cider vinegar
1 teaspoon whole cloves
3½ cups peeled pumpkin cubes,
** (¾-inch pieces)**

1. Combine water and sugar in a saucepan. Place over medium heat and cook, stirring, until dissolved. Then boil for 5 minutes without stirring.

2. Add vinegar, cloves and pumpkin. Simmer for about 1 hour or until pumpkin is tender and translucent but not mushy.

3. Cool and chill before serving. Keep refrigerated. (Makes 2 pints)

Tomatoes

Second only to cucumbers for pickling, tomatoes can be put up green or ripe. Any variety will do, as well as any size. Cherry types are easier to handle in pickling. Tomatoes are super mixers with other vegetables in relishes and sauces.

Spiced Green Tomato Pickles

4 quarts green tomatoes
** (about 24 to 28 medium)**
2 cups onions (about 6 to 8 medium)
½ cup salt
2 green bell peppers, finely chopped
3 cups white or brown sugar
2½ tablespoons celery seed
2½ tablespoons mustard seed
Tie in a bag:
2 tablespoons each whole cloves
** and allspice**
3 sticks cinnamon

1 quart distilled white vinegar
** (approximately)**

1. Wash tomatoes and cut into slices or quarters.

Turn an abundant crop of zucchini squash into "Bread and Butter Pickles" (recipe above).

53

Tomatoes—both green and ripe, mature or miniature—can be turned into quite a variety of condiments from green dills to catsups.

2. Peel onions and slice.

3. Sprinkle alternate layers of tomatoes and onions with salt. Cover and let stand overnight.

4. In the morning drain thoroughly. Put in a kettle and add peppers, sugar, loose spices and spice bag. Add enough vinegar to cover the mixture.

5. Bring to a boil and simmer 15 minutes, or until vegetables are tender.

6. Pack into hot, sterilized jars. Cover with liquid. Seal. Process 5 minutes. (Makes 5 pints)

Note: The pickles may be given a very fresh taste when served by adding a little celery cut into small pieces.

Kosher Style Dill Green Tomato Pickles

Small green firm tomatoes
6 cloves garlic, peeled
6 stalks celery, cut in 2-inch lengths
6 green bell peppers, quartered
2 quarts water
1 quart distilled white vinegar
1 cup salt
Fresh dill to taste
Hot peppers to taste

1. Wash tomatoes and pack in sterilized jars.

2. Add to each jar 1 clove of garlic, 1 stalk of celery and 1 green pepper quarter.

3. Make a brine of the water, vinegar and salt. Boil with the dill for 5 minutes.

4. Pour the hot brine over the pickles in the jar. Seal. Process 5 minutes.

5. These will be ready for use in 4 to 6 weeks. (Makes 6 quarts)

Moroccan Hot Herb & Tomato Relish

2 cups ripe tomatoes, coarsely chopped
¼ cup minced parsley
1 green bell pepper, seeded and chopped
1 cup chopped hearts of celery
¼ cup drained capers
¼ preserved lemon, rinsed and chopped—(see page 68)
8 hot peppers (pickled or fresh)
½ teaspoon salt
½ teaspoon fresh black pepper
Juice of ½ lemon
¼ cup olive oil

1. Mix all the ingredients together in a bowl and refrigerate for several hours before serving. (Makes 1 quart)

Green Tomato Relish

"You need a big kettle and it's a good recipe to do with a neighbor. By yourself it's a little easier to halve it. It's worth the work—it's very good."

½ **lug (wooden crate) green tomatoes**
2 **heads cabbage**
2 **heads cauliflower**
4 **bunches celery**
1½ **dozen large sour pickles**
6 **large bell peppers (preferably 3 red and 3 green, seeds removed)**
6 **large yellow onions**
1 **cup salt**
8 **pounds sugar**
1 **gallon distilled white vinegar**
2 **cups all-purpose flour**
3 **tablespoons dry mustard**
3 **tablespoons turmeric**
  Water to moisten

1. Wash, drain, grind and mix vegetables. Squeeze out moisture. Add salt, sugar and vinegar. Boil for 10 minutes.

2. Mix flour, mustard and turmeric with water and stir until smooth. Stir the flour paste into the vegetable mixture and boil for 10 minutes longer, stirring constantly. (It scorches easily).

3. Pack into sterilized jars, seal and process for 10 minutes.

Hotel Copely Relish

1 **quart green tomatoes, finely chopped**
½ **cup salt**
1 **quart ripe tomatoes, finely chopped**
5 **small yellow onions, chopped**
3 **red bell peppers, finely chopped**
2 **green bell peppers, finely chopped**
1¾ **cup distilled white vinegar**
1 **cup sugar**

1. Cover green tomatoes with ½ cup salt. Let stand 12 hours. Drain.

2. Combine with remaining ingredients in a large kettle. Cover and simmer 30 minutes. Pack into hot, sterilized jars. Seal. Process 5 minutes. (Makes 4 to 5 pints)

Piccalilli

6 **pounds green tomatoes (18 to 20)**
1 **large green bell pepper (seeds removed)**
1 **hot red pepper (seeds removed)**
1 **cup salt**
6 **cups distilled white vinegar**
2 **cups sugar**
½ **teaspoon ground ginger**
½ **teaspoon ground cinnamon**
1 **tablespoon mustard seed or dry mustard**
½ **cup freshly grated or bottled horseradish**

1. Chop coarsely, or slice the tomatoes and peppers.

2. Sprinkle with salt. Cover with water and let soak overnight.

3. Combine vinegar, sugar, ginger, cinnamon and mustard.

4. Drain tomatoes and peppers thoroughly. Simmer gently (do not boil) in vinegar mixture 3 to 4 minutes, or until tender.

5. Add horseradish and heat through.

6. Pack into hot, sterilized jars. Seal. Process 5 minutes.

Note: If desired, ½ teaspoon ground allspice or ground cloves and 1½ pounds sliced onions may be added. Combine onions with tomatoes and peppers before salting. (Makes 5 pints)

Tomato Sauce

4 **quarts peeled, cored, chopped tomatoes (about 2 dozen large)**
3 **cups chopped onions**
2 **cups chopped celery**
1½ **cups chopped green bell peppers, seeds removed (about 3 medium)**
1 **tablespoon salt**

1. Combine all ingredients in a large kettle. Cook until tender. Press through a food mill.

2. Cook pulp until thick—about 1½ hours, stirring frequently to prevent sticking.

3. Pour into hot, sterilized jars. Seal. Process 5 minutes. (Makes 9 half-pints)

Chili Sauce

4 **quarts tomatoes, peeled and chopped**
2 **cups red bell pepper, chopped**
1 **cup green bell pepper, chopped**
1 **cup hot pepper, chopped**
2 **cups onion, chopped**
2 **tablespoons celery seed**
1 **tablespoon mustard seed**
1 **bay leaf**
1 **teaspoon whole cloves**
1 **teaspoon ground ginger**
1 **teaspoon ground nutmeg**
2 **sticks cinnamon**
3 **cups distilled white vinegar**
1 to 1½ **cups sugar (to taste)**
2 **tablespoons salt**

1. Combine tomatoes, sweet peppers, onion and hot pepper.

2. Put celery seed, mustard seed, bay leaf, cloves, ginger, nutmeg and cinnamon in a cheesecloth bag. Add to tomato mixture with vinegar, sugar and salt. Bring to boil; simmer until thick, about 1 to 2 hours, stirring frequently to prevent sticking.

3. Pack into hot, sterilized jars. Seal and process in boiling water bath 15 minutes.

Shirley Sauce

12 **large ripe tomatoes**
2 **large onions**
2 **large green bell peppers**
2 **cups sugar**
2 **cups distilled white vinegar**
2 **tablespoons salt**

1. Peel and chop tomatoes and onions. Remove seeds from peppers and chop.

2. Combine all ingredients in a large kettle and simmer for 1 hour, or until thick.

3. Pack into hot, sterilized jars. Seal. Process 5 minutes. (Makes 6 half-pints)

Tomato Catsup

18 **pounds tomatoes or 7 quarts purée**
3 **tablespoons salt**
⅔ **cup sugar**
1 **tablespoon paprika**
¼ **teaspoon cayenne**
1 **tablespoon dry mustard blended with enough tomato juice to make a paste**
Tie in a bag:
1 **tablespoon whole black peppercorns**
1 **tablespoon whole allspice**
1 **tablespoon mustard seed**
4 **bay leaves**
4 **chilies (small, hot peppers)**
1 **tablespoon dried basil**
2 **cups vinegar**

1. Cook tomatoes until soft, then press pulp through a sieve.

2. Add all remaining ingredients except vinegar to the purée. Cook until thickened, about 1½ hours.

3. Add vinegar during last 10 to 15 minutes of cooking.

4. Remove spices.

5. Pour into hot, sterilized jars. Seal. Process 10 minutes. (Makes 6 to 8 pints)

Turnips

A pickled turnip is not only a taste treat but a delightful texture to bite into. They can be used interchangeably with rutabagas in any of the following recipes.

Pickled Turnips

4 **cups turnips, peeled and cubed**
2 **cups distilled white vinegar**
1 **tablespoon mixed pickling spice**
2 **cloves garlic, peeled**
1 **tablespoon grated horseradish**
1 **teaspoon salt**

1. Pack turnips in quart jars.

2. Combine remaining ingredients and pour over turnips. Seal. Process 10 minutes.

3. Let stand in the refrigerator for 4 weeks before using. (Makes 4 quarts)

Presto Turnip Overnight Pickles

  Presto turnips, peeled, cut into cubes to fill quart container
2⅔ **cups water**
1 **tablespoon salt**
  Distilled white vinegar to cover
2½ to 5 **tablespoons sugar (to taste)**
  Bits of red pepper or chopped pimento

1. Score top and bottom of turnip cube with knife to allow quicker penetration of vinegar and sugar.

2. Soak in water and salt for about 30 minutes to 1 hour.

3. Remove and soak overnight in vinegar and sugar solution. Add red pepper or pimento before serving. (Makes 1 quart)

Sauerruben (Fermented Turnip)

10 pounds purple top turnips, peeled and shredded
¾ cup salt

1. Mix turnips and salt in a crock. Weight down the mixture with a plate (see Sauerkraut, page 35.)

2. The plate should be almost submerged in 24 hours; if not add brine in the ratio of ½ cup salt to 3 cups water.

4. Fermentation will be completed in 15 to 20 days.

5. Pack into jars, seal and process according to directions for sauerkraut. See page 35. (Makes 3 quarts)

Kabees El Lift
(Arabian Pickled Turnip)

Enough small turnips to fill 1 quart jar
2 cups water
1 small beet, peeled and sliced
1 cup white vinegar
4 cloves garlic, minced
2 teaspoons salt

1. Wash turnips and cut off tops and bottoms. Make cuts from the top to ½ inch from the bottom every ¼ inch. Soak in water overnight and wash well in the morning.

2. Pack into a jar with the beet slices.

3. Combine remaining vinegar, garlic and salt and pour cold over vegetables. Store in a cool place. The pickle will be ready in 3 days. (Makes 1 quart)

Takuanzuke

This Japanese version of pickled turnip can be done with radish, cucumber, or cabbage.

1 pound white turnip-root including leaves
2 tablespoons salt

1. Soak turnip in water overnight.

2. Cut into strips (like wide noodles). Cut greens in 1-inch sections.

3. Rub salt into the greens and place in a crock. Lay turnip strips over greens in layers, sprinkling with salt as you lay them in.

4. Cover vegetables with a plate weighted down with a very heavy object. Pickling is completed in 6 to 8 hours.

5. Serve vegetable cold with sauce —see recipe below. (Makes about 1½ cups)

Takuanzuke Sauce

3 tablespoons light soy sauce
3 tablespoons distilled white vinegar
2 tablespoons shredded fresh ginger root
1 small hot red pepper, very finely minced
1½ teaspoons fresh lemon juice

1. Combine all ingredients. Store in refrigerator. (Makes about ⅔ cup)

Mixed vegetables

The possibilities are limitless. Combine two or three vegetables with similar tastes and textures or startle your palate with vivid contrasts. Raid your garden or supermarket and pickle an array of vegetables— capture a garden in a jar.

Combinations for relishes are endless. The next few pages should get you started.

Mixed Mustard Pickles

2 quarts cucumbers, cubed
2 small onions, chopped
5 or 6 stalks celery, chopped
1 cauliflower (about 2 pounds), separated into flowerets and sliced lengthwise ¼-inch thick
2 cups green tomatoes, cubed (about 3 or 4)
2 green bell peppers, cut in lengthwise strips (seeds removed)
2 quarts water
¼ cup salt
½ cup all-purpose flour
½ cup sugar (white or brown)
2½ tablespoons dry mustard
1 tablespoon turmeric
4½ cups distilled white vinegar
1 tablespoon celery seed

1. Combine vegetables, water and salt. Let stand overnight. Drain well. Place in large kettle.

2. Mix together flour, sugar, mustard and turmeric. Gradually stir in enough vinegar (about ¾ cup) to make a paste. Add remaining vinegar. Bring to a boil.

3. Add celery seed and boil for 5 minutes, stirring constantly to prevent lumping.

4. Add drained vegetables. Bring to a boil and simmer for about 15 minutes, or until vegetables are tender. Add additional vinegar if vegetables are not covered with liquid.

5. Pack hot into hot, sterilized jars. Seal at once. Process 10 minutes. (Makes 7 pints)

Dietetic French Pickles

1 quart carrots, peeled and chopped
1 quart celery, finely chopped
1 quart small lima beans
1 quart small green cucumbers, finely chopped
1 quart corn, cut from cob
1 quart yellow onions, finely chopped
1 quart green tomatoes, thinly sliced

½ quart red bell peppers, finely chopped (seeds removed)
½ cup white mustard seed
½ ounce turmeric
1 ounce celery seed
Distilled white vinegar

1. Cook each vegetable separately in boiling salted water until vegetables are barely tender.

2. Season to taste with salt. Drain well. Mix together in a large kettle and add mustard seed, turmeric and celery seed. Mix thoroughly.

3. Cover with vinegar and let come to a boil, stirring frequently.

4. Pack into sterilized jars. Seal. Process in boiling water bath for 10 minutes. (Makes about 12 pints)

Chrystine's Marinated Mixed Vegetables

1 head cauliflower, broken into flowerets
1 red bell pepper, cut into strips (seeds removed)
4 stalks celery, cut into thin strips
1 large red onion, sliced
1 cup small button mushrooms
3 yellow crookneck or zucchini squash, sliced
3 carrots, peeled and cut into julienne strips
1 turnip, peeled and diced
1 cup diced jicama (optional)

Marinade:

½ cup salad oil
1½ cups white wine vinegar
⅓ cup sugar
1 tablespoon salt
1 tablespoon fresh oregano leaves or ¾ teaspoon dried
1 teaspoon pepper
2 teaspoons garlic juice

1. Mix raw vegetables in large container.

2. Blend marinade and pour over vegetables. Let stand overnight.

3. Will keep 1 month refrigerated. (Makes about 4 pints)

Jardiniere

An extremely decorative way to pickle mixed vegetables as illustrated on the title page of this book.

The vegetables are chosen and arranged according to color more than taste, and packing the jar is the most important step.

Some of the vegetables can be packed raw, others need blanching and still others should be parboiled before being put in the jar. When enough layers are built up to fill the jar, the hot vinegar is poured over them and the jar is sealed.

A great Italian dinner begins with a tray of antipasto, meaning "before the pasta."
(recipe on page 58)

Possible vegetables to use are: RAW cucumber, zucchini, sliced green tomato, green cherry tomatoes, green and red peppers, Jerusalem artichoke. BLANCHED quartered onion, okra, cabbage, pimiento peppers.

PARBOILED whole white onions, mushrooms, small eggplants, cauliflower, broccoli, carrots, wax beans and green beans. For each quart of vinegar use:

½ cup salt
1 cup sugar
3 tablespoons mixed pickling spice, tied in a bag

Bring the solution to a boil, remove the spice bag and pour over the arranged vegetables. If a half-gallon or gallon jar is used you may need a double or triple batch of vinegar to fill the jars to the top.

Chow Chow

1 pound small white onions (about 2½ cups)
⅔ cup salt
2 green bell peppers
1 red pepper, sweet or hot
1 pound small cucumbers
1 pound small green tomatoes (6 to 8)
1 pound string beans (about 3½ cups)
1 medium-sized cauliflower
5 or 6 stalks celery
2⅔ cups water
7 tablespoons dry mustard
2 teaspoons turmeric
1 cup sugar
⅔ cup all-purpose flour
5⅓ cups distilled white vinegar

1. Slice onions. Sprinkle with ⅓ cup salt and add enough water to cover.

2. Remove seeds from peppers and chop. Sprinkle with ⅓ cup salt and add enough water to cover.

3. Let onions and peppers stand 24 hours.

4. Then chop remaining vegetables into medium-sized pieces.

5. Drain brine from onions and peppers and add the 2⅔ cups of water to brine. Parboil all vegetables in the diluted brine about 5 minutes. Drain and discard the liquid.

6. Make a paste by mixing mustard, turmeric, sugar and flour with a little vinegar. Bring the remaining vinegar to a boil and add to paste.

7. Stir until smooth, then pour over the drained vegetables and simmer for 20 minutes.

8. Pack into hot, sterilized jars. Seal. Process 5 minutes. (Makes 8 pints)

Catahoula Chow Chow

1 quart green tomatoes, chopped
3 green bell peppers, chopped (seeds removed)

10 small cucumbers, chopped
6 stalks celery, chopped
3 yellow onions, chopped
1 small cabbage, thinly sliced
2 quarts boiling water
¾ cup salt
2 quarts white distilled vinegar
4 tablespoons mustard seed
1 ounce turmeric
1 tablespoon ground allspice
1 tablespoon ground black peppercorns
1 tablespoon ground cloves

1. Combine the chopped vegetables and cover with boiling water, mixed with salt. Let stand for 1 hour. Rinse well with cold water.

2. Bring vinegar and spices to a boil and then add the vegetables. Cook until almost tender, stirring occasionally.

3. Pack into hot, sterilized jars. Seal. Process 5 minutes. (Makes 10 pints)

Antipasto

1 pound celery, sliced
1 pound pearl onions, peeled
1 pound carrots, peeled and sliced
1 pound cauliflower, sliced
1 pound wax beans, cut in 1-inch pieces
1 pound artichoke hearts, trimmed
1 quart water
1 quart vinegar
2 quarts tomato purée
2 cups olive oil
1 tablespoon black peppercorns
½ pound small mushroom caps
1 pound green olives
½ cup capers
2 cups small sour gherkins
¾ cup hot red pickled peppers
2 quarts red wine vinegar
3 cans (6 or 7 ounces each) solid pack tuna
Anchovies (optional)

1. Boil the vegetables in a brine composed of water and vinegar for 10 minutes. Drain and let stand overnight.

2. Combine tomato puree, oil and peppercorns. Simmer for 10 minutes.

3. Add all the ingredients, except tuna and anchovies and cook 10 minutes longer.

4. Pack into hot, sterilized jars and divide the tuna and anchovies among the jars, submerging it in the sauce. Wide flat-sided jars allow you to arrange the vegetables in a beautiful pattern. If necessary add boiling water to fill jars completely. Seal. Process 20 minutes.

5. Let stand 1 month before using. (Makes 10 pints)

Quick Relish

2 cups sauerkraut
1 large green bell pepper
1 large onion
4 ounces pimento
1½ cups celery
1½ cups sugar

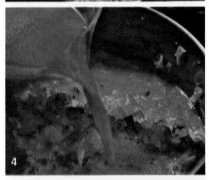

Chow Chow: 1. Prepare fresh vegetables according to recipe. 2. Parboil all vegetables in diluted brine. 3. Make a paste of dried spices, flour and vinegar. 4. Pour spicy solution over drained vegetables and simmer slowly. 5. Pack into hot, sterilized jars and process 5 minutes.

1. Chop first five ingredients.

2. Cover with sugar. Do not stir. Let stand overnight.

3. Put in sterilized jars. Seal. Keep stored in refrigerator. (Makes 3 pints)

Salsa

1 pound onions
2 pounds hot chilies
5 pounds tomatoes
2 teaspoons salt
½ teaspoon pepper
⅓ cup lemon juice or distilled white vinegar

1. Peel and chop onions into small pieces Chop chilies (seeds removed).

2. Peel and chop fresh tomatoes, or chop canned, whole peeled tomatoes into small pieces.

3. Add onions, chilies and other ingredients to chopped tomatoes.

4. Pack into hot jars and process in boiling water bath for 5 minutes. Or bring to a boil and pack into hot, sterilized jars. Seal. Process 5 minutes. (Makes 6 pints)

Note: To increase or decrease hotness of the salsa, increase or decrease the amount of chilies in the recipe. Fresh chilies are "hotter" than pickled, canned, or glass-packed chilies. Either can be used, but fresh chilies give better flavor.

Pepper-Onion Relish

4 cups onions, finely chopped
2 cups red bell peppers, finely chopped
2 cups green bell peppers, finely chopped
1 cup sugar
1 quart distilled white vinegar
4 teaspoons salt

1. Combine all ingredients and bring to a boil.

2. Cook until slightly thickened (about 45 minutes), stirring occasionally.

3. Pack into hot, sterilized jars. Seal. Process in boiling-water bath for 5 minutes. (Makes 5 half-pints)

Dixie Relish

1 head cabbage (3 pounds)
6 medium-sized white onions
6 large red bell peppers
6 large green bell peppers
½ cup salt
1 tablespoon whole cloves
1 tablespoon whole allspice
1 stick cinnamon
4 tablespoons mustard seed
3 tablespoons celery seed
1 quart distilled white vinegar
3 cups sugar
1 tablespoon salt

1. Grind vegetables and mix with salt. Let stand 4 hours.

2. Drain in a clean white cloth, pressing to remove excess liquid.

3. Tie cloves, allspice and cinnamon in bag.

4. Combine vegetables, spice bag and other ingredients and simmer 10 minutes. Remove spice bag.

5. Pour into hot, sterilized jars. Seal. Process 5 minutes. (Makes 5 pints)

India Relish

4 large green bell peppers
4 large red bell peppers
12 green tomatoes
6 cucumbers (6 inches long)
2 large onions
6 tablespoons salt
2 cups chopped cabbage
2 small hot peppers
2½ cups sugar
3 cups distilled white vinegar
3 tablespoons mustard seed
1 teaspoon turmeric
½ teaspoon ground mace
1 teaspoon ground cinnamon
2 teaspoons freshly grated ginger root
3 bay leaves (1 teaspoon crushed)

1. Remove seeds from peppers. Put peppers, tomatoes, cucumbers and onion through food chopper, using coarse blade. Stir salt into vegetables. Let stand overnight.

2. Next morning place vegetables in a colander and force out as much brine as possible.

3. Mix cabbage with other vegetables. Add sugar, vinegar and spices. Mix well and heat to boiling. Boil 3 minutes.

4. Pack into sterilized jars. Seal and process in boiling-water bath for 5 minutes. (Makes 8 pints)

End-of-the-Garden Sauce

8 large apples, peeled, cored and quartered
16 large ripe tomatoes, peeled
6 large red bell peppers
5 medium-sized onions
1 teaspoon ground cinnamon
½ teaspoon ground cloves
1 teaspoon celery seed
½ teaspoon freshly ground black pepper
2 cups cider vinegar
3 cups sugar

1. Using the coarse blade of a food chopper, grind the apples and vegetables.

2. Put them in a heavy kettle with the rest of the ingredients and bring to a boil, stirring constantly.

3 .Cook, stirring constantly, until mixture is thick.

4. Pour into hot, sterilized jars and seal. Process 5 minutes. (Makes 8 pints)

Rummage Relish

½ cup salt
2 quarts chopped green tomatoes
1 quart chopped cabbage
1 quart chopped ripe tomatoes

3 cups chopped onion
2 cups chopped celery
2 green bell peppers, seeded and chopped
2 red bell peppers, seeded and chopped
1 cup chopped cucumber
2 quarts distilled white vinegar
4 cups brown sugar, packed
1 tablespoon celery seed
1 tablespoon mustard seed
1 tablespoon ground cinnamon
1 teaspoon ground ginger
½ teaspoon ground cloves
3 cloves garlic, minced

1. Salt the vegetables and let stand overnight. Drain off as much liquid as possible.

2. Combine the vinegar, sugar and spices in a large kettle and bring the mixture to a boil.

3. Add the vegetables to the vinegar mixture and cook for 30 minutes.

4. Pour into hot, sterilized jars and seal. Process 5 minutes. (Makes 8 pints)

Carrot and Cucumber Relish

8 carrots, ground
6 onions, ground
12 medium-sized cucumbers, peeled and ground
3 green bell peppers, ground
2 small hot red peppers, ground
½ cup coarse salt
4 cups cider vinegar
4 cups sugar
2 teaspoons mustard seed
2 teaspoons celery seed

1. Place the vegetables in a large crock in layers, sprinkling the salt between each layer.

2. Let stand overnight. The next day drain well.

3. Put the rest of the ingredients in a kettle and bring to a boil. Add the vegetables and simmer 15 minutes.

4. Pour into hot, sterilized jars and seal. Process 5 minutes. (Makes 6 pints)

Old English Relish

3 cups finely chopped tomatoes (green or ripe)
3 cups finely chopped onions
3 cups finely chopped celery
4 red bell peppers, finely chopped
4 green bell peppers, finely chopped
4 hot peppers, finely chopped
1 cup horseradish
1 cup whole mustard seed
2 cups sugar
1 cup salt
6 cups white distilled vinegar
2 teaspoons whole pickling spice

1. Combine all ingredients and simmer for 15 to 20 minutes, stirring often.

2. Pack in hot, sterilized jars and seal. Process 5 minutes. (Makes about 6 pints)

Chutney

The mention of "chutney" makes mouths water for spicy East Indian delicacies. However, chutney—a spicy concoction of fruits with herbs and spices—is equally at home with barbecued meats, hamburger, fowl, chops or cold cuts or the same way fruit preserves are used.

Mille's Apple Chutney

20 to 30 apples, finely sliced
1 quart white distilled vinegar
3 pounds brown sugar, packed
2 pounds seedless raisins
1 freshly grated ginger root
6 large cloves of garlic, minced
6 or 8 hot chili peppers, finely chopped
1 teaspoon salt

1. Combine all ingredients in large kettle. Cook slowly until apples turn brown, about one or two hours.

2. Pour into hot, sterilized bottles. Seal and process for 20 minutes.

Note: Chili peppers give a hot taste. Decrease amount of peppers accordingly.

Apple Chutney

12 medium-size tart green apples
6 green tomatoes
4 small white onions
3 large green bell peppers, seeds removed
1 cup seedless raisins
2 tablespoons mustard seed
2 cups sugar
1 quart distilled white vinegar
2 teaspoons salt

1. Peel and cube the apples. Chop the tomatoes, onions and green peppers.

2. Mix with other ingredients. Cook slowly about 1 hour or until of desired consistency.

3. Pack into hot, sterilized jars. Seal at once. Process 5 minutes. (Makes 6 pints)

Apricot-Cherry Chutney

3 pounds apricots, peeled and halved
2 pounds sour cherries, stoned
1 pound dark raisins
2 red bell peppers, seeded and chopped
3 onions, chopped
2 cups cider vinegar
2 cups sugar
½ teaspoon white pepper
Juice of 2 oranges
2 tablespoons minced orange peel
1 tablespoon salt
1½ tablespoons ground nutmeg

East Indian lamb curry dinner features condiments of Mixed Nutty Pickles (page 73), Apple Chutney (page 61), chopped egg, scallions and Lemon Pickle (page 68).

1. Combine all ingredients in a large pot. Cook slowly about 30 minutes, or until desired consistency.

2. Pack into hot, sterilized jars. Seal.

3. Process in boiling-water bath for 20 minutes. (Makes 4 pints)

Black Chutney

1 pound Damson plums (about 20)
2 cups dark corn syrup
½ cup cider vinegar
½ pound seedless raisins (1¼ cups)
10 prunes, cooked and pitted
1 apple, cored and diced
1/16 teaspoon cayenne
½ teaspoon *each* ground allspice, cloves, pepper, cardamon and ginger

1. Cover plums with water and cook until soft. Remove pits.

2. Combine pitted plums with remaining ingredients.

3. Cook slowly about 30 minutes, or until desired consistency is reached.

4. Pack into hot, sterilized jars. Process in boiling water for 20 minutes. (Makes 3 to 4 half-pints)

Note: Guava may be used in place of Damson plums.

Cranberry-Almond Chutney

2 pounds cranberries, washed and picked over
1 pound dried apricot halves, cut in half
6 red onions, peeled and chopped
6 white onions, peeled and chopped
3 green bell peppers, seeded and chopped
1 pound seedless raisins
Juice and grated peel of 2 lemons
6 cups white wine vinegar
4 cups sugar
2 cups whole blanched almonds
1 teaspoon salt
2 teaspoons ground cloves
½ teaspoon white pepper

1. Combine all ingredients, except nuts, in a large saucepan. Bring to a boil, cover and simmer for 30 minutes, stirring often.

2. Add nuts and simmer about 20 minutes longer, or until desired consistency is reached.

3. Pack into hot, sterilized jars. Seal. Process in boiling-water bath 5 minutes. (Makes 4 pints)

Indian Chutney

3½ quarts peeled diced tart apples
3½ cups golden raisins
2 quarts cider vinegar
4 cups sugar
1 cup sliced ginger root
20 dried small hot chili peppers (remove seeds)
8 cloves garlic
6 tablespoons salt
¾ cup mustard seed
1 pint canned cocktail onions

1. In a large stainless steel or porcelain kettle combine apples and raisins with 1 quart vinegar and boil until apples are very soft. Cool.

2. Combine sugar with remaining quart vinegar and boil until soft ball stage (235 degrees). Cool.

3. Put ginger, chili peppers and garlic through fine food chopper, blend in salt and mustard seed.

4. Combine all ingredients except onions and boil 30 to 40 minutes, stirring constantly. Add onions about 10 minutes before completion.

5. Pack into hot, sterilized jars. Seal. Process 5 minutes. (Makes 7 to 8 pints)

Lemon Chutney

Juice and slivered peel of 15 lemons
6 onions, chopped
1 pound white currants
2 green peppers
2 hot red peppers
8 large peaches, skinned and chopped
4 cups sugar
1½ teaspoons ground coriander
1 teaspoon ground fenugreek
1½ teaspoons ground clove
2 teaspoons salt

1. Combine all ingredients and simmer slowly for about 45 minutes. Mash slightly.

2. Pack into hot, sterilized jars. Seal. Process for 5 minutes. (Makes about 6 pints)

Lime Chutney

2 large limes
¼ pound finely chopped suet
6 tart apples, peeled, cored and diced
¼ cup finely chopped candied ginger
2 cups currants
2 cups sugar

1. Halve limes, squeeze juice and chop skins. Mash skins in about 1-inch water until mushy.

2. Lightly brown suet and add other ingredients. Cook very slowly about 25 to 35 minutes until desired consistency is reached.

3. Pack into hot, sterilized jars. Seal. Process 5 minutes. (Makes 4 pints)

Mango Chutney

1 cup distilled white vinegar
3¼ cups sugar
6 cups green mango slices (about 10 medium)
¼ cup freshly grated ginger root
1½ cups seedless raisins
2 chili peppers (seeds removed), finely chopped
1 clove garlic, finely chopped
⅓ cup sliced onion
½ teaspoon salt

1. Boil vinegar and sugar 5 minutes.

2. Add remaining ingredients and cook about ½ hour, or until thick and of desired consistency.

3. Pack into hot, sterilized jars. Seal. Process 5 minutes. (Makes 8 half-pints)

Peach Chutney

3 pounds peeled and chopped peaches
¾ cup cider vinegar
¼ cup fresh lemon juice
1 cup seedless raisins
½ cup chopped white onion
¼ cup slivered preserved ginger
1 tablespoon salt
1 teaspoon ground allspice
½ teaspoon ground cloves
½ teaspoon ground ginger
3 pounds sugar
1 bottle liquid fruit pectin

1. Combine ingredients in a large pot. Cook slowly until desired consistency is reached.

2. Mash slightly before filling hot, sterilized jars. Seal. Process 5 minutes. (Makes about 3 to 4 pints)

Papaya Chutney

2 papayas, pared, seeded and chopped (4 cups)
¼ cup chopped onion
4 apples, pared, cored, chopped (2 cups)
½ cup raisins
¾ cup distilled white vinegar
1 cup brown sugar packed
3 tablespoons lime juice
½ cup water
2 tablespoons green chile peppers, chopped and seeded
1 tablespoon freshly grated ginger root
2 cloves garlic, crushed
1 teaspoon salt
¼ cup slivered blanched almonds

1. In a large kettle, combine papaya, onions, apple, brown sugar, vinegar, raisins, lime juice, water, chilies, ginger, garlic and salt.

2. Cover and simmer for 30 minutes, stirring frequently.

3. Add nuts. Cook uncovered for 30 minutes more, stirring to prevent sticking.

4. Mash slightly and pack in hot, sterilized jars. Seal. Process 10 minutes. (Makes 4 half-pints)

Pear Chutney

8 cups peeled, cored and diced pears (preferably Bartlett)
1 pound light brown sugar
2 cups cider vinegar
1 onion, chopped
1 cup seedless raisins
2 ounces minced crystallized ginger
2 cloves garlic, minced
1½ teaspoons cayenne pepper
2 teaspoons salt
1 teaspoon ground cinnamon
1 teaspoon ground cloves
2 teaspoons mustard seed

1. Mix all ingredients and cook over low heat until desired consistency is reached. About 30 minutes.

2. Pack into hot, sterilized jars. Seal and process 5 minutes. (Makes about 2½ pints)

Pineapple Chutney

1½ cups cider vinegar
1½ cups light brown sugar
4 cups chopped fresh pineapple
1 pound seedless raisins
1 tablespoon salt
2 tablespoons chopped fresh ginger root
2 tablespoons minced garlic
3 hot peppers, seeded and minced
1 cup chopped unsalted macadamia nuts

1. Boil vinegar and sugar 5 minutes.

2. Add all ingredients, except nuts, and cook about ½ hour.

3. Add nuts. Mix well. Pack into hot, sterilized jars. Seal and process 5 minutes. (Makes 4 pints)

Rhubarb Chutney

8 cups sliced rhubarb
7 cups sliced onion
2½ cups golden seedless raisins
7 cups light brown sugar
4 cups cider vinegar
2 tablespoons salt
2 teaspoons ground cinnamon
2 teaspoons ground ginger
1 teaspoon ground cloves
¼ teaspoon cayenne

1. Combine all ingredients in a heavy saucepan. Cook slowly until desired consistency, about 30 minutes.

2. Pack into hot, sterilized jars. Seal. Process 5 minutes. (Makes about 3 pints)

Sweet-Hot Chutney

1 orange, peeled
3 medium apples, cored
2 peaches, nectarines, or mangoes, peeled and seeded
1 lemon, peeled
1 onion, peeled
2¼ cups sugar
1 cup distilled white vinegar
1 cup water
Tie in a bag:
1 teaspoon *each* whole peppers, whole allspice, mustard seed, whole cloves and celery seed
2 chilies, seeded and chopped
⅓ cup sliced blanched almonds (about 50)

1. Chop fruit and onion into small pieces.

2. Combine the sugar, vinegar, and water. Tie in a cheesecloth bag the peppers, allspice, mustard seed, cloves and celery seed. Add bag and chilies.

3. Mix fruit and onion with syrup. Cook 20 minutes. Add almonds and continue cooking 10 minutes longer, or until desired consistency.

4. Remove bag of spices.

5. Pack into hot, sterilized jars. Process in boiling-water bath for 20 minutes. (Makes 4 half-pints)

Note: If desired, more lemon may be used. About 1/16 teaspoon cayenne may be added for a hotter chutney. One-half teaspoon ginger may be added also.

Tomato Chutney

24 medium-sized ripe tomatoes
6 medium-sized onions
3 red bell peppers (seeds removed)
3 green bell peppers (seeds removed)
12 tart apples, cored
1 pound seedless raisins
1 cup celery, finely chopped
2 quarts distilled white vinegar
3 cups brown sugar, packed
1½ tablespoons salt

1. Chop vegetables and apples into ½-inch pieces. Place in large pot.

2. Add remaining ingredients.

3. Cook until thick and clear.

4. Pour into hot, sterilized jars and seal. Process 5 minutes. (Makes about 7 pints)

Worthy's Chutney

1 pint white distilled or cider vinegar
2½ teaspoons whole cloves
2 teaspoons ground ginger
1 teaspoon allspice
1½ teaspoons ground nutmeg
3 pounds onions, chopped
6 pieces garlic, chopped
1 cup raisins
1 cup currants
6 or 7 pieces candied ginger, thinly sliced
5 peaches, thinly sliced crosswise
5 nectarines, thinly sliced crosswise
¾ large firm cantaloupe, thinly sliced

1. Mix vinegar and spices and boil 30 minutes.

2. Add onion, garlic, raisins, currants and candied ginger. Cook 15 minutes more.

3. Add fruit, cook until clear and thick, being careful not to burn.

4. Fill hot, sterile jars. Seal and process 5 minutes.

Note: Fresh ginger can be used in place of candied. Wash and soak 4 or 5 pieces of root overnight. Cook until tender or until there is just a little water left. Peel, slice thin and use the remaining liquid also, adding it to the mixture.

To make Apple Chutney: 1. Peel and chop apples and vegetables. 2. Combine seasonings, vinegar and vegetables and simmer until desired consistency. 3. Pour into hot, sterilized jars and seal. 4. Process in boiling water bath for 5 minutes. (See pages 24 and 25).

Fruits

The imaginative pickler can capture an orangerie in a jar—everything from the old favorite peaches, pears and apples to exotic mangoes and papayas.

Sweet Apple Relish

    4 pounds apples, peeled, cored and
        sliced thin
    3 quarts water with 4 tablespoons
        vinegar
    1¼ cups distilled white vinegar
    1 cup sugar
    ½ cup light corn syrup
    ⅔ cup water
    1½ teaspoons whole cloves
    2 sticks cinnamon, broken up
    1 teaspoon whole allspice

1. Soak apples in vinegared water.

2. Boil ingredients and add drained apples. Simmer for 3 minutes.

3. Pack fruit into hot, sterilized jars and cover with syrup. Seal. Process 5 minutes. (Makes 4 pints)

Apple-Tomato Butter

    10 McIntosh, Pippin or other tart
        apples, peeled, cored, and ground
    8 onions, peeled and ground
    6 green bell peppers, ground
        (seeds removed)
    8 small hot green peppers, ground
    16 large ripe tomatoes, peeled and
        chopped
    3 cups sugar
    2½ cups cider vinegar
    3 tablespoons salt
    2 teaspoons ground cinnamon
    2 teaspoons ground cloves

1. Put all the ingredients in a large kettle and bring to a boil.

2. Cook over low heat, stirring to prevent sticking, until the mixture is thick and dark, about 2 hours.

3. Pour into hot, sterilized jars and seal. Process 5 minutes. (Makes 5-6 pints)

Spiced Bananas Hawaii

    12 greenish bananas
    1½ cups lime juice
    2¼ cups sugar
    6 tablespoons butter
    1 teaspoon ground cloves
    6 sticks cinnamon
    1 tablespoon chopped fresh or
        crystallized ginger
    1 teaspoon salt
    1 teaspoon ground nutmeg
    ¾ teaspoon ground mace

1. Peel bananas and cut into 1-inch pieces.

2. Combine remaining ingredients in a saucepan and bring to boil.

Tropical fruit pickles are perfect for a luau or family dining. Left to right: Bananas Hawaii (above), Pineapple Chutney (page 62), Pickled Papayas (page 70) and Spiced Mangoes (page 68).

3. Add bananas and simmer 5 minutes.

4. Remove bananas. Place in sterilized jars and seal at once. Process 10 minutes. (Makes 3 or 4 pints)

Pickled Sliced Bananas

    1 pound brown sugar
    1½ cups cider vinegar
    1½ teaspoons ground mace
    1½ teaspoons ground cinnamon
    ½ teaspoon ground clove
    12 bananas

1. Boil the sugar, vinegar, and spices for 10 minutes.

2. Peel bananas and cut in diagonal slices 1-inch thick. Add the fruit to the syrup and cook for 5 minutes.

3. Pack fruit and syrup into sterilized jars and seal. Process 10 minutes. (Makes 4 pints)

Spiced Banana Relish

    1 tablespoon cloves
    3 cinnamon sticks
    1½ teaspoons allspice, whole
    1 nutmeg, broken with hammer
    2 cups cider vinegar
    ½ cup sugar
    16 ripe bananas

1. Tie spices in a cheesecloth bag. Combine vinegar and sugar in a saucepan, add spice bag and simmer until mixture starts to thicken.

2. Peel and cut the bananas in ½-inch slices. Add bananas to syrup and simmer for 2 minutes. Remove spice bag and pack relish in hot, sterilized jars. Seal immediately. Process 10 minutes. (Makes about 4 pints)

Sweet Pickled Banana Spears

    4 cups sugar
    1 cup distilled white vinegar
    1 teaspoon ground mace
    2 cinnamon sticks, broken up
    2 teaspoons whole cloves
    12 large, almost ripe bananas

1. Dissolve sugar in vinegar and bring to a boil with the spices.

2. Peel the bananas and quarter them lengthwise. Add them to the syrup and boil about 5 minutes or until they can be easily pierced with a fork. Cool in the syrup.

3. Pack fruit on end in quart jars then fill with syrup and seal. Process 10 minutes. (Makes about 4 pints)

Spiced Blueberries

    4 quarts blueberries
    2 cups distilled white vinegar
    3 pounds brown sugar
    1 tablespoon whole allspice
    2 cinnamon sticks
    1 teaspoon whole cloves

1. Wash and drain berries.

2. Boil vinegar, sugar, and spices for 5 minutes. Add berries. Simmer

about 3 minutes or until berries are tender. Let stand overnight.

3. Using a slotted spoon pack the berries in hot, sterilized jars. Boil the syrup 2 minutes and pour over. Seal. Process 10 minutes. (Makes 8-10 pints)

Cantaloupe Pickles

    2 medium-sized underripe cantaloupes
    1 quart distilled vinegar
    2 cups water
    1 teaspoon ground mace
    2 sticks cinnamon
    2 teaspoons ground cloves
    4 cups sugar (or 2 cups granulated and
        2 cups brown sugar)

1. Peel cantaloupe and cut flesh into 1-inch pieces. Discard peelings.

2. Combine vinegar and water. Bring to a boil. Add spices. Spices may be tied loosely in a thin, white cloth, if they are to be removed later.

3. Place the melon pieces in a non-metal container. Pour boiling vinegar solution over them. Let stand overnight.

4. Pour vinegar off into a saucepan and bring to a boil.

5. Add sugar and melon. Simmer until clear, about 1 hour.

6. With a slotted spoon pack cantaloupe into hot, sterilized jars.

7. Bring vinegar mixture to a boil. Boil to make a medium syrup.

8. Pour boiling syrup over cantaloupe. Seal. Process 5 minutes. (Makes 4 pints)

Cherry Olives

    2 pounds firm, ripe Royal Ann or
        black cherries
    4 teaspoons salt
    4 teaspoons sugar
    2 cups vinegar

1. Wash cherries. Either stem and pit or leave whole. Prick with needle.

2. Fill hot, sterilized jars with cherries.

3. Add 1 teaspoon salt, 1 teaspoon sugar, and ½ cup vinegar to each jar. Fill to top with cold water and seal. Process 5 minutes.

4. Refrigerate and let stand about 1 month before using. (Makes 4 pints)

Pickled Sour Cherries

    4 quarts sour cherries
    4 tablespoons salt
    Equal parts of cold water and
        distilled white vinegar

1. Wash the cherries well without removing stems.

2. Pack into sterilized quart jars, adding one tablespoon salt to each quart of cherries.

3. Fill the jars with equal parts of cold water and vinegar. Seal. Process 5 minutes. (Makes 4 quarts)

Crabapple Relish

2 cups cider vinegar
4 cups brown sugar
½ teaspoon ground cinnamon
1 tablespoon whole cloves
1 tablespoon ground nutmeg
7 pounds crabapples, cored and diced
2 pounds seedless raisins
3 oranges, peeled, seeded and diced

1. Heat the vinegar, sugar and spices in a large kettle, stirring to dissolve the sugar. Bring to a simmer.

2. Add the fruits and cook about 10 minutes, or until apples are tender but not mushy.

3. Pack into hot, sterilized jars. Seal. Process 15 minutes. (Makes 6 pints)

Crabapple Pickles

1 gallon crabapples
4 cups distilled white vinegar
6 cups sugar
2 cups water
2 sticks cinnamon, broken up
1 teaspoon whole cloves
1 tablespoon whole allspice

1. Wash apples and pierce their skins in several places with a skewer. Steam them for 10 minutes over rapidly boiling water.

2. Combine vinegar, sugar and water and bring to a boil. Put the spices in a cheesecloth bag and boil them in the combined liquids for about 10 minutes.

3. Add the apples and cook until tender. Do not overcook them.

4. Pack apples in hot, sterilized jars and cover them with the boiling syrup. Seal and process in a boiling-water bath for 10 minutes. (Makes 3 quarts)

Pickled Crabapples

2 quarts crabapples
3 cups distilled white vinegar
3 cups water
6 cups sugar
1 tablespoon whole allspice
1 stick cinnamon
1 tablespoon whole cloves
1 tablespoon blade mace

1. Wash crabapples. Do not peel.

2. Mix together vinegar, water, sugar and spices. Boil until syrup coats a spoon.

3. Add apples. Reheat slowly to avoid bursting the skins and simmer until apples are tender.

4. Pack apples into hot jars.

5. Cover with boiling syrup and seal. Process 15 minutes. (Makes 6 pints)

Cranberry Pickle Sauce

4 cups cranberries
Juice of 1 lemon
1½ cups sugar
¾ cup distilled white vinegar
1 cinnamon stick broken in pieces
1 teaspoon ground cloves
1 teaspoon ground nutmeg

1. Wash berries and bring them to a boil with lemon juice, sugar and vinegar. Cook gently until the berries burst.

2. Add the spices and cook 15 minutes longer, until mixture is thick.

3. Turn into hot, sterilized jars and seal. Process 15 minutes. (Makes 2 pints)

Pickled Figs I

Baking soda
5 pounds figs with stems
2 cups distilled white vinegar
7 cups sugar
2 cinnamon sticks, broken up
1 clove for each fig

1. Sprinkle a handful of baking soda on the figs and cover them with boiling water. Let stand for 10 minutes and wash thoroughly.

2. Boil remaining ingredients 15 minutes. Add the fruit and bring to a rolling boil. Boil for 15 minutes. Let stand 24 hours.

3. Repeat boiling for 15 minutes on the next two days and after the third boiling, pack the fruit and liquid in hot, sterilized jars. Seal. Process 10 minutes. (Makes 5 pints)

Pickled Figs II

3 quarts whole figs
2 quarts boiling water
1 cup water
2 teaspoons *each:* whole pickling spices, whole cloves and stick cinnamon (broken)
6 cups brown sugar
1 cup vinegar

1. Cover figs with boiling water and allow to stand for 5 minutes.

2. Make syrup from next four ingredients. Tie spices in a cheesecloth bag and add to syrup.

3. Drain figs. Boil in syrup 3 consecutive days for 10 minutes each day, then pack into sterilized jars.

4. Seal and process in boiling-water bath for 10 minutes. (Makes 6 pints)

Fruit Relish

3 large peaches
3 large firm pears
4 medium-sized red tomatoes
1 green bell pepper
3 small onions
¾ cup sugar
1½ cups white wine vinegar
2 teaspoons salt

¼ teaspoon ground cinnamon
¼ teaspoon ground cloves
⅛ teaspoon cayenne

1. Peel, core and/or seed fruits and vegetables.

2. Put them through the food chopper using medium blade.

3. Add remaining ingredients and cook on lowest heat until mixture thickens, about 2 hours.

4. Turn into hot, sterilized pint jars, add ½ cinnamon stick and 2 whole cloves to each bottle and seal. Process 5 minutes. (Makes 3 pints)

Spiced Gooseberries

This relish can also be made with red currants.

2 cups cider vinegar
2½ pounds light brown sugar
1 tablespoon each ground allspice, ground cloves, ground nutmeg and ground cinnamon
2 teaspoons salt
4 pounds gooseberries

1. Put all the ingredients, except the berries, in a kettle and gradually bring to a boil stirring to dissolve the sugar. Boil 5 minutes.

2. Add the berries and simmer until they are quite tender, about 30 minutes.

3. Pour into hot, sterilized jars and seal. Process 10 minutes. (Makes 3 pints)

Gooseberry Catsup

2 cups cider vinegar
2 tablespoons ground cloves
2 tablespoons ground cinnamon
2 tablespoons ground allspice
5 quarts gooseberries
4 pounds sugar

1. Boil vinegar and spices.

2. Add the berries and sugar and boil gently, stirring occasionally for 1 hour.

3. Pour into hot, sterilized jars and seal. Process 15 minutes. (Makes 3 quarts)

Pickled Green Grape Bunches

8 medium bunches of grapes, about 6 pounds
1½ quarts cider vinegar
10 cups sugar
1 tablespoon whole cloves

1. Grapes should not be over-ripe. Leave them on the stems and wash

Pickled fruits and berries create a mid-winter still-life: (clockwise from top) Pickled Grape Bunches (above). Fig Pickles (above), Spiced Gooseberries (above), Pickled Crabapples (above) and Cherry Olives (page 65).

them carefully. Pack them into clean quart jars, leaving enough room so as not to bruise them.

2. Boil vinegar and sugar with the cloves for 5 minutes, then pour over the grapes filling the jars. Seal. Process 10 minutes. (Makes 4 quarts)

Spiced Red Grapes

2 cups distilled white vinegar
1 teaspoon ground nutmeg, ground ginger, ground cinnamon and ground cloves
8 cups sugar
10 pounds red or purple grapes, stemmed and seeded

1. Heat the vinegar and spices in a kettle. Dissolve the sugar in the liquid and bring to a boil. Cook for 5 minutes.

2. Add the grapes and cook until thick.

3. Pour into hot, sterilized jars and seal. Process 10 minutes. (Makes 8 pints)

Pickled Grapes

4 pounds seedless grapes
1 cup sugar
2 cups water
1 cup distilled white vinegar
1 tablespoon chopped fresh ginger root
1½ tablespoons whole cloves
2 pieces cinnamon stick

1. Wash grapes and remove stems.

2. Combine remaining ingredients and heat until sugar is dissolved.

3. Add grapes and cook slowly until tender.

4. Pack into hot, sterilized jars. Seal. Process 10 minutes. (Makes 4 pints)

Grape Catsup

4 cups grapes, peeled, skins reserved
4 cups cider vinegar
6 cups sugar
2 tablespoons ground cinnamon
2 tablespoons ground cloves

1. Cook the grapes in a saucepan until they are tender. Push them through a sieve to remove seeds.

2. Combine the grapes, vinegar, sugar and the reserved skins. Bring to a boil and simmer for 30 minutes.

3. Add the spices and boil 10 minutes longer.

4. Turn into hot, sterilized jars and seal. Process 10 minutes. (Makes 3 pints)

Pickled Kumquats

2 quarts kumquats
2 tablespoons baking soda
Water
4 cups sugar
1 cup distilled white vinegar
1 stick cinnamon

1. Clean kumquats, rinse well. Place in colander, sprinkle with soda. Turn into a large pan. Pour over boiling water to cover. Let stand 10 minutes. Drain and run cold water over fruit to rinse well.

2. Slit each kumquat on one side. Place in large pan and cover with clear water. Boil about 10 minutes. Drain.

3. Combine sugar with an equal amount of clean water. Add vinegar and cinnamon. Bring to boil. Add kumquats. Boil slowly until fruit is transparent and syrup is thickened.

4. Place kumquats in hot, sterilized jars. Pour in syrup. Seal.

5. Process in boiling-water bath 5 minutes. (Makes 6 pints)

Moroccan Preserved Lemons

20 thin skinned lemons
Kosher salt
Olive oil

1. Score the lemons in quarters, cutting through the skin from the top to ½ inch from the bottom.

2. Sprinkle a layer of salt on the bottom of a quart jar. Take the lemons, one at a time, squeeze the juice into the jar, put some salt inside the skin and then press it down into the jar. After each lemon is packed sprinkle the outside with salt as well. (Additional lemons may be needed to fill the jar.)

3. Pour enough olive oil into the jar to cover the lemons. Seal the jar tightly and store in a cool place for at least 2 weeks.

Note: This is used as an ingredient in Moroccan cooking. It may be added to marinades, salad dressings and many fish recipes.

Lemon Pickle

Another relish for Indian dinners

1 pound lemons, cut in wedges, lengthwise
¼ cup salt
5 cloves garlic, finely minced
5 tablespoons crushed hot red pepper, pods and seeds
3 cups salad oil

1. Salt the lemon wedges on all sides and pack into a quart jar. Cover the jar and let stand for 4 days at room temperature.

2. Add the garlic and pepper, mixing them through the lemons.

3. Heat the oil in a saucepan until very hot and pour it over the lemons. Cool. Cover and let stand another 4 days at room temperature.

4. Pack into hot, sterilized jars. Process 5 minutes.

Pungent Pickled Mango

1 dozen firm mangoes
1 quart distilled white vinegar
1 clove garlic, minced
1 tablespoon salt
5 tablespoons sugar
Spice bag:
2 tablespoons mustard seeds
3 tablespoons chopped fresh ginger root
3 tablespoons chopped fresh horseradish
12 black peppercorns

1. Peel and seed mangoes and cut into slices. Pack into hot, sterilized jars.

2. Boil the remaining ingredients for 20 minutes. Remove the spice bag and pour the hot syrup over the fruit. Seal. Process 15 minutes. Pickle will be ready in 1 month. (Yield: 4 pints)

Spiced Mangoes

4 cups sugar
2 cups cider vinegar
1 cup water
2 tablespoons whole cloves
3 cinnamon sticks
1 tablespoon whole allspice
2 bay leaves
3 tablespoons orange peel, minced
8 pounds mangoes, peeled and sliced

1. Put all the ingredients, except the mangoes, in a kettle. Bring to a boil.

2. Add the fruit and simmer just until the fruit begins to turn translucent.

3. Let stand until the following day then bring to a boil again. Turn into hot, sterilized jars and seal. Process 20 minutes. (Makes 5 pints)

Orangerie (Spiced orange slices)

12 oranges
3½ cups distilled white vinegar
4 cups sugar
15 whole cloves
4 cinnamon sticks
2 teaspoons blade mace

1. Wash oranges and place in pot with enough water to cover. Bring to boil, cover and simmer until peeling is tender.

2. Drain, reserving liquid. Cool oranges by plunging into cold water. Cool and slice very thin, about ⅛-inch thick.

3. Combine vinegar, sugar and 2½ cups of reserved liquid. Tie spices in a bag and add. Bring to boil and simmer 10 minutes. Add orange slices, return to boil. Simmer slowly for 30 minutes.

Spiced Orange Slices are tangy garnishes for drinks. Pickled Kumquats are a natural accompaniment.

4. Pour into bowl, cover and let stand at room temperature 24 hours.

5. Drain orange slices and pack into hot, sterilized jars. Remove spice bag and return syrup to the pot. Bring to boil and boil until thickened. Pour over oranges. Cool. Seal when cold. Process 5 minutes. (Makes 4 pints)

Note: Keep stored two months before using.

Green Papaya Relish

8 cups grated green papaya, unpeeled
⅓ cup papaya seeds, mashed
3 tablespoons chopped fresh ginger root
¼ cup cider vinegar
½ teaspoon salt
Takasio sauce to taste (Available at oriental grocers)

1. Combine all ingredients. Allow to mellow for 24 hours at room temperature. Pack in covered jar.

2. Refrigerate. Keeps well for 2 weeks. (Makes 4 cups)

Pickled Papayas

4 cups green papaya
2 cups water
2 cups sugar
1 cup distilled white vinegar
4 whole cloves
1 cinnamon stick
2 bay leaves
6 black peppercorns

1. Peel and slice papayas, discarding seeds. Boil in water for 3 minutes. Drain and reserve.

2. Combine sugar and vinegar. Bring to boil.

3. Add spices and bring to boil again. Add papaya and cook over medium heat, 10 to 12 minutes. (Stir carefully to avoid breaking fruit.)

4. Pour into hot, sterilized jars. Seal. Process 20 minutes. (Makes 2 pints)

Stuffed Pickled Peaches

16 freestone peaches, peeled
½ cup chopped walnuts
¼ cup chopped raisins
2 tablespoons honey
1 teaspoon ground cinnamon
½ teaspoon ground nutmeg
6 cups sugar
2 cups cider vinegar
2 cups water
18 whole cloves

1. Remove stones from peaches through stem end, leaving them whole.

2. Mix nuts, raisins, honey, cinnamon and nutmeg. Fill the cavities in the peaches with the mixture. Arrange the fruit, open side up, in a large skillet.

3. Boil the remaining ingredients in a pot and carefully pour the liquid over the peaches. Simmer for 8 min-

utes, or until the peaches are just cooked through.

4. Pack the peaches in hot, sterilized jars and pour the syrup over them. Seal. Process 10 minutes. (Yield: 4 pints)

Pickled Peaches, Pears or Apricots

4 quarts small peaches, pears or apricots
Whole cloves
⅓ ounce stick cinnamon (about six 3-inch pieces)
8 cups sugar (4 cups granulated and 4 cups brown sugar may be used, or all brown sugar)
1 quart vinegar

1. Dip the peaches quickly into hot water—slip skins on freestones or peel clings.

2. Stick each peach with 4 cloves. Or, put cloves loosely in a clean cheesecloth bag.

3. Boil spices, sugar and vinegar together for 2 minutes.

4. Put peaches into syrup and boil gently until soft, using half the quantity of peaches at a time.

5. Pack into hot, sterilized jars. Seal. Process 10 minutes. Pears and apricots may be prepared in the same way omitting the dip in hot water. The pears may be peeled. (Makes 3 quarts)

Note: Less sugar may be used for a more tart pickle. Two sliced lemons are a nice addition to the syrup of spiced pears.

Brandied Peach Pickles

2 cups cider vinegar
5 cups sugar
2 cinnamon sticks, broken
2 tablespoons cassia buds
½ teaspoon oil of clove
24 small peaches
4 cinnamon sticks
4 whole cloves
4 tablespoons brandy

1. Combine the first 5 ingredients in a pot and bring to a boil.

2. Remove skins from peaches by dropping for 1 minute in boiling water, then sliding the skins off under cold water.

3. Put 1 cinnamon stick and 1 clove in each bottle; then pack the peaches.

4. Strain the hot vinegar over the peaches and add 1 tablespoon brandy to each jar. Seal. Process 10 minutes. (Yield: 4 pints)

Pear Relish

Excellent hamburger spread or a tangy compliment to cold meats.

8 cups ground pears
2 cups ground onion
6 green or red bell peppers, ground

Peeled, whole pears are steeped in spicy liquid, then poured into hot, sterilized jars. (Recipe above).

1 ground hot pepper or 1 tablespoon
   hot pepper sauce
4 ground dill pickles
3 tablespoons dry mustard
1 quart white wine vinegar
¼ cup flour
1 tablespoon turmeric
2 tablespoons salt
2 cups sugar

1. Mix all ingredients and stir well.

2. Bring to rolling boil over medium-high heat. Cook 15 minutes.

3. Pack in jars and seal. Process 5 minutes. (Makes 7 pints)

Lucy's Hot Pear Relish

1 peck pears or 4 quarts prepared pears
5 pounds onions
10 green bell peppers (seeds removed)
4 red bell peppers (seeds removed)
6 small hot peppers (seeds removed)
4 cups sugar
2 tablespoons turmeric
5 tablespoons salt
6 tablespoons dry mustard
3 pints distilled white vinegar

1. Peel and grind pears in food grinder using medium blade.

2. Grind onions and peppers and add to the pears. Set aside.

3. Mix sugar, turmeric, salt and mustard in a large kettle. Add vinegar and stir until sugar is dissolved. Heat until boiling.

4. Add pears and vegetable mixture and bring to boiling. Simmer 25 minutes.

5. Pour into hot, sterilized jars. Seal. Process 5 minutes. (Makes 6 quarts)

Spiced Plums

4 quarts plums
6 cups sugar
1 cup distilled white vinegar
1 teaspoon ground cinnamon
1 teaspoon ground allspice
½ teaspoon ground cloves

1. Prick each plum with a fork to prevent the skins from bursting.

2. Boil sugar, vinegar and spices together for several minutes, then pour over the plums in a large crock. Let stand 24 hours.

3. Repeat next day.

4. The third day pack the plums into sterilized jars. Bring the syrup to a rolling boil and pour over the plums. Process 10 minutes. (Makes 4 quarts)

Southern Plum Catsup

4 pounds purple plums
½ cup water
2 tablespoons ground cinnamon
1½ tablespoons ground cloves
1½ tablespoons ground allspice
1 teaspoon salt
½ teaspoon cayenne
¼ teaspoon white pepper

Another way of pickling pears—grinding for relish (recipe on left).

1½ pounds sugar
1 cup red wine vinegar

1. Wash plums and remove stems. Put them in a pot with the water and cook covered until tender.

2. Put the plums through a colandar to remove seeds.

3. Return plums to the pot and add the remaining ingredients.

4. Simmer slowly until the sauce is quite thick. Pour into hot, sterilized jars and seal. Process 10 minutes. (Makes 4 pints)

Spiced Prunes

1 pound dried prunes
1 quart water
⅛ teaspoon salt
1 cup sugar
8 whole allspice
10 whole cloves
3 cinnamon sticks, broken
¼ cup red wine vinegar

1. Wash prunes and soak overnight in water and salt.

2. Add sugar and spices and boil 15 to 20 minutes.

3. Add the vinegar and cook another 10 minutes; the sauce should be fairly thick.

4. Pack into a jar and refrigerate overnight. (Serves 6)

Prune Catsup

Good with game or poultry.

6 pounds prunes
4 cups sugar
1 tablespoon ground cinnamon
2 teaspoons ground cloves
2 teaspoons ground allspice
¾ cup cider vinegar

1. In a pot cover the prunes with water and simmer until they are very tender. Remove pits and put the prunes through a food mill or blender.

2. Put the prune purée in a heavy kettle with the remaining ingredients. Bring the mixture to a boil and cook, stirring often, until the mixture is thick.

3. Pour into hot, sterilized jars and seal. Process 10 minutes. (Makes 4 pints)

Pickled Watermelon Balls

Also try honeydew, muskmelons, or mixed melons.

    10 cups watermelon balls
     2 quarts cold water
    ½ cup salt
     3 lemons, sliced
    4½ cups granulated sugar
     2 tablespoons crystallized ginger,
        chopped

1. Soak fruit overnight in the water with the salt. Drain and rinse with cold water.

2. Put fruit in a kettle with the lemons, sugar and ginger; and enough water to cover the fruit. Cook slowly until the syrup is clear, about 20 minutes.

3. Pack fruit in hot, sterilized jars, but continue to boil syrup until it threads.

4. Pour the syrup over the fruit and seal. Process 10 minutes. (Makes 3 pints)

Quick Pickled Watermelon Rind

    4 quarts watermelon rind
    2 tablespoons salt
      Boiling water to cover
    1 quart distilled white vinegar
    8 cups sugar
    ¼ cup broken cinnamon stick
    1 tablespoon whole cloves

1. Peel green skin off strips of melon rind and trim off pink portion. Cut in 1-inch squares.

2. Add salt and enough boiling water to cover.

3. Simmer until rind is tender.

4. Drain and chill the rind in very cold water at least 1 hour, or overnight.

5. After rind has chilled, prepare a syrup by boiling together the vinegar and sugar. Tie cinnamon and cloves in a cheesecloth bag and add.

6. Drain rind and place in syrup.

7. Simmer until rind becomes clear and slightly transparent. Remove spices.

8. Pack rind into hot, sterilized jars. Cover with boiling syrup. Seal. Process 5 minutes. (Makes 4 to 5 pints)

Notes on Making Watermelon Pickles

1. A 16-pound watermelon will yield from 5 to 6 pounds rind.

2. One pound rind is equivalent to 1 quart rind and will make about 1 pint pickles.

3. The pink part of the melon will not become crisp.

4. The rind is better if melon is not overripe or is one grown late in the season.

Photos show steps in "Quick Pickled Watermelon Rind" recipe (on left). Remove pulp from sliced watermelon.

Cube rind. Some cooks leave green rind on as shown here, however we found the pickle too tough and suggest peeling.

Add salt and boiling water to cover. Simmer until the rind is tender.

Drain rind and chill in cold water at least an hour, or overnight.

Prepare syrup of vinegar and seasonings. Simmer until rind is clear. Remove spices.

Pack into hot, sterilized jars. Seal and process in boiling water bath for 5 minutes.

Let's pickle something new

Here are some goodies you may not have tried yet. Edible ornamentals—grape leaves, flowers, even a garden "weed"—and some nuts, proving our point that almost anything can be pickled.

Grape Leaves

Whole grape leaves
2 teaspoons salt in 1 quart water
1 cup lemon juice or
2½ teaspoons citric acid
1 quart water

1. Add salt to water and bring to boil. Add grape leaves and let blanch for 30 seconds.

2. Drain. Form into loose rolls and pack vertically in pint jars.

3. Add lemon juice or critric acid to water. Bring to boil, then pour over rolls of leaves in jar.

4. Seal. Process in boiling-water bath for 15 minutes.

Pickled Petals

Flowers and buds of roses, violets, nasturtium, chrysanthemum, calendula, primrose, day-lilies, gladiolus or geraniums
Sugar
Distilled white vinegar
Mace or mint sprigs

1. Carefully remove sepals from base of flower, stems and stamens (pollen producer) from inside of flowers. Layer flowers in a crock or jar, covering each layer with sugar.

2. When jar is filled, pour boiling vinegar to fill. Add a sprig of mace or mint.

3. Seal. Pickled petals are ready to mix with salads or garnish a relish tray in about 4 to 5 days. Keep refrigerated.

Note: Use home-grown flowers that are free from insect blight or garden sprays. Pick in the early morning

Day Lily Dillies

2 pounds day lily buds
5 hot red pepper pods
5 cloves garlic
1 quart distilled white vinegar
½ cup water
6 tablespoons salt
1 tablespoon celery seed
1 tablespoon mustard seed

1. Wash and drain lily buds. Pack neatly in 5 hot, sterilized pint jars. Put 1 pepper pod and 1 whole garlic clove in each jar.

2. Bring the remaining ingredients to a boil and pour the liquid over the lily buds. Seal. Process 10 minutes. (Makes 5 pints)

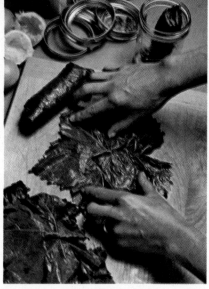

Grape leaves are rolled for easy storage.

False Capers
(Pickled nasturtium buds)

Green nasturtium buds
1 cup salt
2 quarts water
Distilled white vinegar

1. Cover buds in salt-water brine. Weight down to keep immersed. Allow to cure 24 hours.

2. Remove buds from brine. Soak in cold water for 60 minutes. Drain.

3. Bring vinegar to a boil.

4. Pack buds in hot, sterilized jars. Cover with boiling vinegar. Seal.

5. Process in boiling-water bath 10 minutes.

Mixed Nutty Pickles

2 teaspoons whole cloves
2 cinnamon sticks
1-inch piece ginger root
4 cups distilled white vinegar
4 cups honey
1 tablespoon salt
4 cups shelled walnuts, halved
2 cups shelled pecans, halved
2 cups shelled cashew nuts
2 cups peanuts
or any other nuts available

1. Tie spices in bag and place in pot with vinegar, honey and salt. Bring to boil, stirring. Simmer for 15 minutes.

2. Add mixed nuts and simmer 15 minutes longer. Remove spice bag.

3. Pour into hot, sterilized jars. Seal. Process 20 minutes. (Makes 6 pints)

Hot Pickled Walnuts

3 cups unripe (still green) walnuts
Brine: **½ cup salt to 1 quart water**
1 quart cider vinegar
2 tablespoons freshly ground pepper
1 tablespoon salt
1½ teaspoon ground allspice
1 teaspoon cayenne
1 teaspoon Tabasco

1. Prick each nut with a skewer in several places and soak them in brine 1 week.

2. Rinse nuts, place in pot with fresh batch of brine and simmer gently for 10 minutes.

3. Drain off liquid and arrange on a flat surface. Let nuts stand for several days or until they turn black.

4. Boil the rest of the ingredients for 10 minutes.

5. Pack hot, sterilized jars with walnuts. Fill jars with boiling pickling liquid. Seal. Process 15 minutes. (Makes 2 pints)

Sweet Pickled Walnuts

2 cups white wine vinegar
2 cups light brown sugar
1 cinnamon stick, broken
1 teaspoon whole cloves
½ teaspoon salt
6 cups shelled walnut halves

1. Put all the ingredients, except walnuts, in a kettle and bring to a boil, stirring to dissolve the sugar. Simmer for 15 minutes.

2. Add walnuts and simmer gently for 15 minutes longer.

3. Turn into hot, sterilized jars and seal. Process 20 minutes. (Makes 4 pints)

Hot Spiced Peanuts

An excellent condiment with curry dinners.

5 cups shelled roasted peanuts
3 bay leaves, broken
2½ cups distilled white vinegar and
½ cup water
2 hot red peppers, minced (seeds removed)
4 cloves garlic, minced
2 teaspoons chili powder
1 teaspoon cayenne
1 tablespoon mustard seed
¼ cup sugar
1½ tablespoons salt

1. Rinse nuts in warm water, drain and pack them in hot, sterilized jars.

2. Combine other ingredients in a pot. Bring mixture to a boil and simmer 5 minutes.

3. Pour boiling liquid over nuts, filling jars. Seal. Process 20 minutes. (Makes 3 pints)

Pecan Relish

4 cups shelled pecan halves
Juice and minced peel of 2 oranges
Juice and minced peel of 1 lemon
1 cup seedless raisins
1½ cups white wine vinegar
2½ cups brown sugar, packed
½ teaspoon salt
1 tablespoon grated nutmeg
½ teaspoon ground coriander
1 teaspoon ground cinnamon

1. Place all ingredients into kettle and slowly bring to boil, stirring constantly to dissolve sugar.

2. Simmer for 20 minutes or until citrus peel is tender and liquid is clear.

3. Turn into hot, sterilized jars and seal. Process 20 minutes.
(Makes 3 pints)

Purslane Pickles

A garden weed transformed into sweet-sour condiment.

2 quarts purslane stems, cut into strips
3 cups onions, peeled and thinly sliced
3 cups brown sugar, packed
1 cup cider vinegar
2 teaspoons salt
Spice bag:
2 tablespoons mixed pickling spices
2 cloves garlic
2 tablespoons broken cinnamon sticks
1 tablespoon chopped fresh ginger root

1. Mix all ingredients and cook gently until purslane stems are tender. Remove spice bag.

2. Pack into hot sterilized jars. Seal. Process 15 minutes.
(Makes about 3 pints)

Eggs

Pickled eggs are not only fun to prepare but are very attractive in the pantry, as gifts, or on the table. They are great with meats at a cold buffet. Turn them into deviled eggs, or salad, or hot dishes, or garnishes.

Most recipes call for using beet juice when you want to color eggs. But you might experiment with other natural fruit or vegetable juices.

Pickled Eggs with Beets

Beets and eggs to fill jar
1 onion, sliced
3 cups water
½ cup white wine or cider vinegar
2 tablespoons sugar (or to taste)
Salt and pepper (to taste)

1. Wash beets, cook until tender. Chill, peel and slice into a bowl. Slice onions on top.

2. Hard boil eggs, cool and peel.

3. Bring remaining ingredients to a boil. Pour hot mixture over beets and onions, cover with a plate and marinate until cool.

4. Layer beets, onion and eggs in a jar, fill with liquid. Keep in refrigerator.

Spiced Pickled Eggs

1 dozen hard boiled eggs, peeled
3 cups white vinegar
1 tablespoon minced ginger root
1 tablespoon minced horseradish root

Today's flower bouquet can be a mid-winter garnish. See Pickled Petals (page 73).

1 teaspoon whole cloves
1 teaspoon whole allspice
1 teaspoon white peppercorns
1 teaspoon salt

1. Pack eggs in a wide-mouthed jar that is sterilized.

2. Combine other ingredients, bring to boil and simmer for 10 minutes.

3. Pour boiling liquid gently over the eggs, filling the jar completely. Seal at once. Process 10 minutes.

Pickled Chinese Tea Eggs

10 to 12 eggs
  Water to cover
3 tablespoons black tea leaves
1 tablespoon salt
Brine:
1 quart distilled white vinegar
4 hot red peppers, minced
  (seeds removed)
1 tablespoon coriander seed
1 teaspoon black peppercorns
1 teaspoon salt
1 teaspoon mustard seed

1. Place eggs in water to cover and bring to a boil over medium heat; then cook gently 5 to 7 minutes. Reserve the water.

2. Cool eggs thoroughly under cold running water for 5 minutes. Then either roll each egg gently on a board or table, or tap lightly with a spoon to crackle the entire shell.

3. Bring the reserved water to a boil again. There should be about 4 cups. If not add more water. Add tea leaves, salt and cracked eggs; then simmer, covered, until egg shells turn brown (about 1 hour).

4. Turn off the heat and let eggs stand, covered, 30 minutes more. Drain eggs, and shell. May be eaten like this or pickled as follows:

5. Place peeled eggs in hot sterile jars and cover with brine that has boiled 15 minutes. Seal and process 10 minutes.

Garlic Pickled Eggs

2 dozen eggs, hard-boiled and peeled
4 sprigs tarragon or
  1 tablespoon dried
8 cloves garlic, slivered
1½ quarts cider vinegar
1 teaspoon mustard seed
2 bay leaves
1 teaspoon cardamon seed
2 teaspoons black peppercorns
2 teaspoons salt
1½ tablespoons sugar

1. Pack the eggs in 4 one-pint jars with one sprig tarragon and 2 cloves garlic in each.

2. Combine remaining ingredients in a pot and bring to a boil. Simmer gently 15 minutes.

3. Strain the hot vinegar over the eggs. Seal. Process 10 minutes.
(Makes 4 pints)

Pickled eggs can be made in many colors and patterns. Top to bottom: Pickled Egg with Beets, Chinese Tea Egg, and Garlic Pickled Egg.

Vinegar-making

It's possible to make your own vinegars in two forms. Either you can go all the way, making your vinegar completely from scratch, or you can flavor a commercial vinegar to your liking.

In simple terms vinegar is the juice of a fruit or of a grain mash that has been naturally fermented. The fermentation produces alcohol which, upon exposure to oxygen, turns into the acid solution we call vinegar. Anyone who's opened a bottle of wine and waited too long to finish it has witnessed the second half of the vinegar making process. The oxygen in the bottle reacted with the alcohol and, "turned" the wine into vinegar.

Distilled white vinegars and brewed malt vinegars should not be made at home because of the apparatus needed for distilling. But fermented fruit vinegars can be homemade.

Making Vinegar from scratch

The most difficult step in vinegar making is the extraction of juices from the fruits used. Apples are the most common source of juice for fruit vinegars, but try pears, peaches, berries or grapes. You'll have to crush the fruit in a fruit press or food mill. A potato masher works for softer fruits.

If you've been canning and want to make vinegar from the leftovers, you can boil the discarded cores and peels in an equal part of water until they're mushy. All the fruit should then be strained through a double layer of cheesecloth. To the dilute juices of peels and cores, add a quarter cup of sugar for each quart of juice (this replaces missing fruit sugars).

You can also start vinegar from unfiltered, unpasteurized fruit juices available in many markets.

Vinegar makers disagree as to whether yeast should be added to the juice; it will hasten the fermentation. Choosing to do so use one-quarter of a cake per quart of cool liquid. Store the jars, three-quarters full and uncapped, but covered with a cloth, in a cool place.

The gas bubbles of the fermentation process will be in evidence for weeks. Once you're *sure* that it's ended, remove any sediment and add

Herbs and spices in unlimited combinations can be used to flavor commercial vinegars either by steeping over heat as shown here or by leaving in cold vinegar for several weeks. See recipes on pages 78 and 79 for ideas.

After vinegar has reached desired flavor strain it into clean bottles and cap tightly.

Twigs or whole pieces of fresh herbs make delicious and visually pleasing vinegars. Simply place washed herbs into a clean bottle, add distilled commercial vinegar, cap tightly and store. Ready to use in about six weeks.

Oregano

Tarragon

Dill

one-half pint of unpasteurized vinegar (available in many "health food" stores) to each quart of juice. This is also a "hastener" but will also prevent spoilage by strongly beginning the vinegar conversion stage. Leave the liquid in a warm place and taste periodically until it reaches the strength you prefer. Then it's time to again remove any sediment plus the white rubbery mass of vinegar bacteria. Strain into bottles and cap the finished product tightly.

Flavored Vinegars

The preparation of flavored vinegars is considerably easier than making vinegar from scratch. It only involves the addition of herbs and spices to a commercially bottled vinegar. Virtually every spice and herb can be used, as you can tell from the following recipes. Try new combinations until you find the flavors you like best.

Herb Vinegar

1 quart distilled white vinegar
4 oz. fresh marjoram, sage, tarragon, or thyme

1. Place the herbs in cold vinegar for five to six weeks. Then remove the herbs by straining the vinegar or leave twigs in the bottles for show.

2. Store in tightly capped bottles.

Fine Wine Vinegar

Leftover fine burgundy or bordeaux wine
Large glass jar

1. After dinner parties, pour leftover wine (even from the glasses) into the jar, cover with layer of cheesecloth to keep out dust particles.

2. Store the jar in a dark warm place, at least 60 degrees. The wine will turn in several weeks.

3. Keep adding wine as you use the vinegar.

Note: It is almost impossible to control the acidity of this vinegar since it changes composition so often. Before you use it, taste it to find if it needs thinning with water or strengthening with additional vinegar or lemon juice.

All Seasons Vinegar

1 teaspoon crushed dill seed
½ teaspoon black pepper
½ ounce dried marjoram
¼ teaspoon *each* whole allspice and whole crushed cloves
¼ ounce *each* dried basil, dried rosemary, dried mint and dried tarragon
2 quarts cider vinegar

1. Add the blended herbs to the vinegar in a covered jar or crock. Stir and crush every day with a wooden spoon.

A vinegar connoisseur can make a collection of flavors to rival the wine cellar.

2. After three weeks, strain, filter and bottle tightly.

Hot Chili Vinegar

24 red chili peppers
1 pint distilled white vinegar

1. Cut the peppers in two and place in a quart bottle. Add the vinegar and let steep for two weeks, shaking the contents up daily.

2. Strain the vinegar through cloth or a fine sieve. This brew is so strong it might be best to store in small bottles, tightly corked.

Mild Chili Vinegar

2 ounces chili peppers
1 teaspoon salt
1 quart distilled white vinegar

1. Large peppers can be cut. Place the peppers in the salted vinegar.

2. Shake the mixture every day for a week and a half, then strain the contents. Place in corked container.

Mint Vinegar

Fresh mint, to fill quart jar
1 quart distilled white vinegar

1. Fill a quart jar loosely with fresh mint leaves. Semi-crush the leaves. Fill the jar with distilled white vinegar, cover, and store in a cool place.

2. After two weeks strain and rebottle. You can also substitute basil for mint in this recipe.

Garlic Vinegar

2 ounces garlic cloves, peeled and minced or crushed
3 teaspoons salt
1 quart distilled white vinegar

1. Combine the ingredients in a bottle and store in a cool place.

2. Shake up the contents periodically. Then strain and rebottle.

Horseradish Vinegar

3 medium-large horseradish roots, freshly scraped
¼ teaspoon cayenne
½ teaspoon each black pepper and celery seed
1 quart distilled white vinegar

1. Combine the ingredients in a 2-quart jar, cover tightly, and steep for 10 days.

2. Strain and rebottle.

Onion Vinegar

1 cup finely chopped Spanish or white onions or 4 ounces sliced shallots
1 quart distilled white vinegar

1. Combine ingredients, cover, and let steep for two weeks.

2. Strain and rebottle.

Rose Vinegar

1 cup rose petals, fresh
1 quart distilled white vinegar

1. Place the petals in the bottom of a quart jar and add the vinegar. Let the jar stand in the sun for two weeks.

2. Strain through a paper filter, rebottle and seal. Heavenly!

Spiced Vinegar (Mild)

2 one-inch sticks cinnamon
4 blades mace
8 peppercorns
12 cloves
15 allspice
1 quart distilled white vinegar

Directions: see next page.

Spiced Vinegar (Hot)

2 tablespoons mustard seed
2 tablespoons allspice
2 tablespoons dried chilies
24 cloves
24 black peppercorns
1 quart distilled white vinegar

Both these recipes can be prepared by the long (cold) and short (hot) methods. If you have planned well-enough ahead, and won't need the vinegar for a few months, the long steeping will produce a finer taste.

Cold Method:

1. Simply add the ingredients to the vinegar, cap the bottle and let stand for six to eight weeks.

2. Shake the bottle occasionally in that time and, of course, strain the contents before rebottling.

Hot Method:

1. Put the vinegar in the top half of a double boiler or a similar-arrangement. Bring the water to a boil then remove from the heat and allow for the spices to steep in the warm vinegar for two hours. You may use a spice bag or allow the spices to float free.

2. Then follow the normal procedure of straining, rebottling and capping tightly.

Berry Vinegar

1 pound berries, (blackberries, black currants, elderberries, mulberries, and raspberries are best)
1 pint distilled white vinegar
Sugar

1. Place only prime condition fruit in a large glass bowl. Add the vinegar and cover with a towel. Steep for three to five days, stirring occasionally.

2. Strain the fruit and, in a saucepan, add up to two cups sugar for each pint of liquid (taste along the way for the desired ratio).

3. Boil the mixture, stirring until the sugar is dissolved and continue boiling for another 10 minutes.

4. Rebottle in hot jars and seal tightly.

Three Spiced Vinegars

I. Tangy

½ cup sugar
1 tablespoon chopped fresh ginger root
1 one-inch stick cinnamon
1 teaspoon *each* finely ground horseradish, mustard seed and mace
1½ tablespoons black peppercorns
2 teaspoons salt
2 cloves garlic, minced
12 whole cloves
1 quart distilled white vinegar

1. Place all ingredients in a saucepan and bring to a boil. Simmer gently for 20 minutes. Remove from heat and cool.

2. Then strain and bottle tightly.

II. Spicy

1 tablespoon mustard seed
1 tablespoon mace
1 tablespoon whole allspice
1 tablespoon grated horseradish
1 bay leaf
1 onion, diced
1 teaspoon salt
1 quart distilled white vinegar

1. Bring all the ingredients to a boil in a saucepan then lower the heat and simmer for four minutes.

2. Strain and bottle.

III. Mild

1 two-inch stick cinnamon
12 whole cloves
Small piece fresh ginger root
1½ pints distilled white vinegar

1. Tie the spices in a spice bag. Place the spice bag in the vinegar and boil for 20 to 25 minutes keeping the lid on the pot.

2. Remove the spice bag and bottle.

Texas A&M Spiced Vinegar

1 tablespoon mustard seed
1 or 2 tablespoons mixed pickling spices
3 hot red peppers
1½ cups sugar
1 cup water
3 cups distilled white vinegar

1. Mix above ingredients and bring to boil. Sugar may be increased or decreased according to taste. Honey or corn syrup could be substituted for sugar (see: ingredients, sugar page 9).

2. Strain and bottle.

Celery Vinegar

1 large bunch of celery
1 quart distilled white vinegar
1 teaspoon salt
1 tablespoon sugar
2 teaspoons celery seed

1. Chop the celery into small pieces; include the leaves and trimmed roots. Place the celery in a large glass bowl. Heat the vinegar and remaining ingredients to boiling and pour them over the celery.

2. Allow to cool then bottle and seal. Steep for twelve days shaking vigorously every day.

3. Strain the contents and rebottle.

Horseradish Vinegar (Cooked)

1 quart distilled white vinegar
1 teaspoon salt
1 teaspoon cayenne
1 cup grated horseradish
2 ounces finely minced shallots or young onions

1. Heat vinegar to boiling and pour over other ingredients, placed in a jar. Cover and place in a warm spot for two weeks.

2. Then strain, boil again and rebottle, sealing tightly.

Cucumber Vinegar

¼ teaspoon cayenne
1 tablespoon salt
6 shallots, chopped
10 small cucumbers, chopped
1 quart distilled white vinegar

1. Place all the ingredients in a saucepan and bring to a boil. Simmer for three to four minutes. Then put into a large jar, cover tightly and let sit for at least a week.

2. Strain the mixture and rebottle the vinegar, sealing carefully.

Onion Vinegar (Cooked)

1 tablespoon brown sugar
1 tablespoon salt
2 peeled and chopped white onions
1 quart distilled white vinegar

1. Add the ingredients and seasonings to the vinegar in a saucepan. Bring the mixture to a boil and remove from the heat immediately.

2. Empty the contents into a jar, seal and leave for two weeks.

3. Then strain the mixture, rebottle and reseal the vinegar.

Honey Vinegar

This is an old Jewish recipe. It's said to make a good quality white vinegar.

1 quart strained honey
8 quarts warm water

1. Mix the honey and water together and let stand in a warm place until fermentation stops.

2. Then seal in canning jars or bottles.

Raspberry Vinegar

From an Early American manuscript cookbook.

Raspberries
Vinegar
Sugar

1. Measure your raspberries into a bowl, and pour over them an equal quantity of vinegar.

2. The next day take out the fruit and add as much more to the same vinegar.

3. The day following, remove the raspberries as before and again replace them with fresh and on the fourth day put to each pint of liquid a pound of sugar—place it in a skillet on a gentle fire, simmer and skim it for a short time when it will be ready to bottle for use.

4. Seal it down well.

Meats

Pickling is probably the best method of safely canning meats at home. Follow directions that come with your pressure-canner for absolute safety. All meat products, pickled or canned, should be refrigerated or stored in a cool place. Unless they are used in a few days, pickled meats must be canned.

Corned Beef

An authentic English method of preservation. Works equally as well for wild game such as venison.

1¼ cups sugar
½ cup sodium nitrate (saltpeter), available from your druggist
1 tablespoon sodium nitrite, available from your druggist
1 tablespoon fresh ground pepper
1 teaspoon ground cloves
3 pounds salt
¼ cup mixed pickling spices
6 bay leaves
1 onion, minced
4 garlic cloves, minced
  Water
  Beef (brisket, chuck or round) or game roast

1. Mix all ingredients, except meat, in crock or glass container. Add water to make a total of 6 gallons. This will corn up to 20 pounds of meat.

2. Place meat into liquid, weight down to keep immersed. Cover. Store in cool place.

3. Leave in the liquid for 15 days, removing the meat and stirring the liquid well every five days. Replace the meat in a reverse position each time.

4. Remove meat from liquid after 15 days. Wrap well. Store in refrigerator or cool place.

5. To cook, place in pan, add water to cover. Bring to boil, remove scum. Simmer until tender. Season to taste.

Kosher Corned Beef or Tongue

2 cups coarse salt
4 quarts water
¼ cup sugar
1 teaspoon sodium nitrate (saltpeter), available from drugstore
2 tablespoons mixed pickling spices
2 teaspoons paprika
12-15 bay leaves
4 cloves garlic
  Beef brisket, round, chuck roast or tongue

1. Dissolve salt in water.

2. Add sodium nitrate, sugar, spices, paprika and bay leaves. Boil 5 minutes. Cool.

3. Place select cut of beef in crock. Add garlic and cover with pickling brine. Weight down.

4. Keep in cool place (around 38 degrees), turning weekly.

5. Remove from brine after three weeks. (Enough brine to pickle 10 pounds of beef)

Spiced Pickled Beef

Boneless beef round, 25 pounds
4 ounces sodium nitrate (saltpeter)
4 cups salt
1 quart black molasses
1 ounce ground nutmeg
2 tablespoons ground cloves
2 tablespoons ground allspice

1. Rub sodium nitrate and a little salt on all surfaces of beef.

2. Mix remaining ingredients and pour over meat in crock. Let stand

Home-pickled Corned Beef is served with traditional boiled vegetables. Condiments include Pickled Peaches (page 70) and Horseradish Relish (page 43).

1. Kosher style Corned Beef begins by pouring cooled, boiled pickling brine over fresh meat in a crock.

2. Place a heavy weight, such as a bottle or bag of water, to keep meat submerged under brine.

3. Remove meat from crock, stir brine, replace meat in reverse position.

4. Remove meat after 3 weeks. Wrap well and refrigerate until ready to cook.

for 3 weeks in a cool place (around 38 degrees). Turn each week.

3. Remove from crock and tie in cheesecloth. Keep cool until ready to cook.

To Cook: Remove cloth, place in a pot, cover with cold water and boil until tender (about 3 hours). Cool in water before serving.

Mince Meat

- 5 pounds apples, cored and chopped
- 5 cups water (boil apple peel and cores or 1 quart sweet cider)
- 2 pounds lean beef, cooked tender and put through food chopper
- ½ pound suet, chopped fine
- 3 pounds raisins, chopped
- 1 tablespoon salt
- 2 cups brown sugar
- 1 cup meat stock
- 2½ pints grape juice
- 1 teaspoon mace
- ½ teaspoon pepper
- 2 teaspoons *each* ground allspice, ground nutmeg, ground cloves and ground cinnamon
- 1 cup molasses
- 1 orange (juice and chopped peel)
- 1 lemon (juice and chopped peel)
- ¾ cup distilled white vinegar

1. Boil apple peelings and cores in 5 cups water and strain or use 4 cups water and 1 cup sweet cider. Add beef, suet, apples, raisins, salt, sugar and stock. Simmer 1 hour, stirring.

2. Add grape juice, spices, molasses, orange juice, peel, lemon juice, peel and vinegar.

3. Allow the entire mixture to come to a boil and boil 10 minutes. Pack into jars within 1 inch of top.

4. Process pints and quarts 25 minutes at 10 pounds pressure. (Makes 10 pints)

Sauerbraten

- 4 pounds beef (brisket or round)
- 2 cups cider vinegar
- 1 teaspoon salt
- ½ teaspoon pepper
- ½ lemon, sliced
- 3 tablespoons sugar
- 3 bay leaves
- 8 whole cloves
- 1 large onion, sliced
- 1 teaspoon black peppercorns
- 1 teaspoon juniper berries

1. In a bowl just large enough to hold the meat, place the meat and all the other ingredients.

2. Refrigerate for about 1 week, turning the meat daily.

3. On the day the dish is to be served, remove the meat from the marinade, dry it, dredge it in flour and sear it in a little fat in the bottom of a heavy dutch oven. Add the marinade and cover the pot.

4. Simmer on the stove or in a 325 degree oven for about 2 to 2½ hours or until the meat is quite tender.

5. Thicken the gravy, if desired, and serve with the sliced meat. (Serves 6 to 8)

Pickled Pigs' Feet

Pigs feet
Salt
Vinegar solution:
2 quarts distilled white vinegar
1 small red pepper
2 tablespoons grated horseradish
1 teaspoon black peppercorns
1 teaspoon whole allspice
1 bay leaf

1. Scald, scrape and clean the feet very thoroughly, then sprinkle lightly with salt and let stand for 4 to 8 hours.

2. Wash the feet well in clean water. Place them in hot water and cook until tender but not until meat can be removed from bones.

3. Pack the feet in jars to within 1 inch of top.

4. Mix vinegar solution ingredients together and bring to the boiling point then fill jars to within ½ inch of top. Seal.

5. Process pints and quarts 75 minutes at 10 pounds pressure.

Everything you need for making mincemeat (recipe above).

Fish

The cuisine of many nations includes pickled or marinated fish as appetizers, snacks, or main courses. Of all forms of pickling these may be among the most interesting, as well as being simply delicious and high in nutritive value. Frozen fish is acceptable for pickling.

Most fish must be kept refrigerated during and after the pickling process.

Inlagd Sil (Swedish pickled herring)

6 salt herring, filleted
3 cups white vinegar
¾ cup sugar
3 red onions, sliced
5 sprigs fresh dill
1 carrot, peeled, sliced
6 black peppercorns
4 bay leaves
2 teaspoons whole allspice, bruised

1. Soak fillets in cold water overnight.

2. Combine other ingredients and bring to boil, stirring until sugar dissolves.

3. Rinse fillets in cold water and arrange them in a small crock. Pour the hot liquid and vegetables into crock, covering the fish.

4. Let stand, refrigerated, at least 1 week before using.

Note: To serve, slice the fish in one-inch sections. Mix a new marinade of vinegar and sugar, with chopped red onion and chopped fresh dill, in the same proportions as the pickling marinade. Arrange the fish on a serving dish and pour the sauce over it. The Swedes accompany this dish with boiled new potatoes and copious amounts of aquavit and beer.

Pickled Herring In Cream

3 herring, filleted
1 cup sliced onion
1 bay leaf
4 black peppercorns
1½ cups white wine vinegar
½ cup boiling water
½ cup sour cream

1. Wash herring, cover with water, and soak overnight in the refrigerator.

2. Cut the fish into 1 inch pieces and arrange alternate layers of onion and fish in a jar or crock.

3. Combine the remaining ingredients and pour over the fish. Chill in refrigerator for at least 3 days.

Herring in Dark Wine Sauce

3 herring, unskinned, cut into 1 inch pieces
1 cup dry red wine

1 cup red wine vinegar
1 cup dark brown sugar, packed
3 bay leaves
3 cloves
4 allspice

1. Place herring in large glass jar.

2. Mix remaining ingredients to make marinade.

3. Pour the marinade over the fish and refrigerate. This can be eaten after 24 hours, but is much better after several days.

Potted Herring

3 herring
2 tablespoons salt
1 teaspoon ground black pepper
4 bay leaves
1 teaspoon *each* whole cloves, black peppercorns and whole allspice
2½ cups white wine vinegar

1. Gut the fish and remove the heads. Wash well, inside and out. Dry. Rub salt and ground pepper into the cavities.

2. Put fish in a small baking dish and scatter spices over them. Pour vinegar over the fish, using more if needed to half cover them.

3. Bake in a 275 degree oven for 2 hours. Cool and refrigerate. The fish will keep 2 weeks.

Crock Pickled Sardines

10 pounds whole small herrings, scaled, washed, gilled and gutted
6 cups distilled white vinegar
2 cups water
2 pounds salt
1 pound sugar
2 tablespoons *each* ground allspice and ground black pepper
1 tablespoon sodium nitrate (saltpeter)
1 tablespoon *each* ground cloves, ground ginger and ground nutmeg
5 bay leaves, broken into pieces

1. Soak the herring in vinegar and water overnight.

2. Combine the salt, sugar and spices.

3. Pour out the brine and drain fish completely. Rub each fish with the salt-spice mixture and pack into crock in neat layers, belly side up. Pack the last layer, back side up and top with remaining salt-spice mixture. Weight down the fish with a plate and heavy object.

4. The brine will rise in several days. Let the fish cure for about 2 weeks before using.

5. The sardines will keep for several months under refrigeration or in cold storage.

Pike or Pickerel Pickle

5 pounds cleaned fillet cut into 2-inch sections
Salt
3 cups white wine vinegar
3 cups water
1 cup chopped onion
2 cloves garlic
1 tablespoon *each* whole allspice and mustard seed
5 bay leaves, broken into pieces
1 teaspoon *each* whole cloves and whole peppercorns
Garnish: 5 bay leaves, peppercorns, sliced onion

1. Dredge the fish pieces in salt and pack them in a crock. Let stand overnight.

2. Rinse off the fish and soak it in fresh cold water for 30 minutes.

3. Combine all other ingredients, except fish and garnish, in a kettle and bring the mixture to a boil. Cook 10 minutes.

4. Add drained fish and cook for 10 more minutes.

5. Distribute the garnish into 5 one-pint jars. Pack in the fish and strain the boiling liquid over it, filling the jars. Seal immediately.
(Makes 5 pints)

Pickled Eel

8 pounds eel, cleaned, skinned, cured and cut into 1-inch chunks
2 cups salt
¼ pound butter
2 cloves garlic, minced
4 onions thinly sliced
2 tablespoons *each* whole allspice, whole cloves, black peppercorns and mustard seed
10 bay leaves
Brine:
2 quarts distilled white vinegar to 2½ cups water

1. Dredge eel with salt and let stand 2 hours. Rinse off the salt and dry the eel.

2. Melt the butter with garlic and brush it on the eel. Broil the eel close to the flame until it is lightly brown on all sides. Drain on paper towel and let cool.

3. Pack the pieces in a crock with the spices and onion slices scattered between the layers. Cover the eel with a weighted plate and let stand 24 hours.

4. Pour the brine over the eel, covering it completely. Let stand 48 hours before using. This will keep for many months in cold storage.

Pickled Shrimp

First brine:
    2 quarts water
    ½ cup salt
    1 cup distilled white vinegar
    2 teaspoons *each* hot red pepper
        and whole white peppercorns
    4 bay leaves
    1 teaspoon *each* whole cloves,
        allspice, mustard seed
    6 pounds shrimp, unshelled, or peeled
        and deveined
    Bay leaves and lemon slices
Pickling brine:
    6 cups water
    3 cups distilled white vinegar
    2 tablespoons sugar
    3 tablespoons mixed pickling spice

1. Bring the first brine to boil and cook for 30 minutes on low heat.

2. Add shrimp. Return to boil and simmer 5 minutes. Remove shrimp and cool. (The first brine may be used again to poach fresh fish or seafood).

3. Pack shrimps into sterilized jars. Put 2 bay leaves and 2 lemon slices in each jar. Fill the jars with the pickling brine to overflowing and seal at once. Refrigerate at least 1 week before using. (Makes 4 pints)

Pickled Fish

    5 pounds pike, pickerel or whitefish
    Salt
    2 cups distilled white vinegar
    2 cups water
    1 teaspoon salt
    8 bay leaves
    16 whole allspice
    20 black peppercorns
    1 teaspoon sugar
    1 lemon, thinly sliced
    5 onions, thinly sliced

1. Cut the fish in 2 inch slices, rub it with salt and chill for 4 hours.

2. Boil the vinegar, water, salt, bay leaves, allspice, peppercorns, sugar, lemon slices and one of the onions for 25 minutes.

3. Remove the lemon and add the fish. Simmer gently until fish is cooked through, about 12 minutes.

4. Fill a large crock with alternating layers of fish and raw sliced onion. Pour the cooking liquid over the fish adding more water if necessary to cover the contents of the crock.

5. Refrigerate for at least one week before serving. The liquid will gel. This aspic is served with the fish and onion.

◁

Pickled fish clockwise from top): Salmon (page 85). Shrimp (page 85), Oysters (page 85), Herring in Cream (page 83), Herring in Dark Wine Sauce (page 83) and Caviar (page 86).

Seviche

    3 pounds fresh, skinned, boned, mild-
        flavored fish such as turbot, white-
        fish, or mackerel, cut into bite-sized
        pieces
    ½ cup lime juice
    1½ teaspoons salt
    ½ cup Spanish olive oil
    ½ teaspoon dried oregano
    1½ cups peeled, seeded tomatoes,
        coarsely chopped
    2 canned hot peppers, minced
        (seeds removed)
    1 tablespoon minced cilantro
    1 onion, chopped
    1 teaspoon freshly ground pepper
    2 large avocados, stoned, peeled
        and cubed

1. Soak the fish in the lime juice overnight in the refrigerator, stirring it occasionally.

2. Next day combine the fish with the remaining ingredients and toss gently. Let stand in the refrigerator until serving time. (Serves 12)

Pickled Oysters

    5 pints oysters
    1 tablespoon salt
    2 cups distilled white vinegar
    2 tablespoons black peppercorns
    2 tablespoons each whole cloves and
        whole allspice
    4 bay leaves
    2 hot red peppers, chopped
        (seeds removed)

1. Cook the oysters in their own liquor on the lowest heat, without boiling, just until their edges curl.

2. Strain the liquor into a pot and combine it with the remaining ingredients. Bring to the boiling point, remove from heat and let stand until the liquid is cool.

3. Pour the cool liquid over the oysters in a crock and let stand overnight in a cool place.

4. Pack the oysters in sterilized jars and seal. Keep stored in refrigerator. (Makes 5 pints)

Marinated Shrimp

    ¼ cup salad oil
    2 tablespoons white wine vinegar
    2 tablespoons prepared brown
        mustard
    1 teaspoon paprika
    ½ teaspoon salt
    ¼ teaspoon red pepper
    1½ pounds boiled shrimp
    ½ cup finely chopped green onions

1. Place all ingredients except shrimp and onions in blender. Mix well.

2. Pour over shrimp and onions. Mix thoroughly.

3. Marinate 24 hours in refrigerator.

Sweet and Sour Fish

    3 pounds pike, carp, or whitefish
    ½ cups brown sugar, packed
    Juice of 1 lemon
    1 onion, chopped
    1 cinnamon stick
    1½ cups raisins
    2 tablespoons sherry
    Salt and pepper to taste

1. Cut the fish in serving pieces and poach it in boiling water until it is cooked through. Put fish on a serving platter.

2. Mix 1 cup of the poaching liquid with the rest of the ingredients and boil about 10 minutes. Pour this sauce over the fish.

3. Refrigerate overnight or until cold. (Serves 6)

Poisson Cru (A Tahitian appetizer)

    2 pounds very fresh fish fillets, sliced
        in long strips (mackerel, tuna,
        snapper, salmon)
    Juice of 10 limes
    1 teaspoon salt
    ¼ cup white wine vinegar
    1 cup salad oil
    1 cup coconut cream (pressed out
        liquor of fresh grated coconut meat)
    1½ teaspoon dry mustard
    1 teaspoon sugar
    1 teaspoon freshly ground pepper
    3 cloves garlic, minced
    1 cup chopped scallions
    ½ cup chopped celery
    3 tablespoons chopped parsley
    1½ cups coarsely chopped tomatoes
    3 hard-boiled eggs, chopped

1. Marinate the fish in the lime juice and salt for 6 hours at room temperature. Drain.

2. Combine the rest of the ingredients and toss gently but thoroughly.

3. Add the fish, tossing lightly and refrigerate overnight.

4. When serving, garnish with tomato and hard boiled egg slices. (Serves 8)

Swedish Pickled Salmon

    4 pound slice of whole salmon
    Twigs of pine or spruce
    3 tablespoons salt
    3 tablespoons sugar
    1 teaspoon white peppercorns, crushed
    3 bunches of fresh dill (about ½ pound)
    4 tablespoons cognac

1. Bone the fish and cut into two fillets. Wipe dry with a cloth.

2. Spread some twigs and ⅓ of the dill on the bottom of a deep, flat dish.

3. Combine the salt, sugar, and pepper. Spread this mixture on the boned side of the fish fillets.

4. Set one fillet skin side down, on the bed of twigs and dill.

How to...

Scale:

Wet the fish and scrape gently toward the head with a serrated fish scaler or the back edge of a knife.

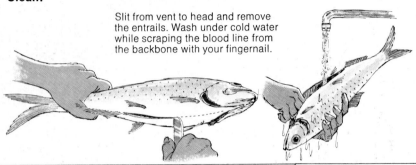

Clean:

Slit from vent to head and remove the entrails. Wash under cold water while scraping the blood line from the backbone with your fingernail.

Remove roe (eggs):

Slit the belly as if for cleaning, being careful not to puncture any of the organs. You'll find the eggs, if any, on each side toward the back. Scrape them into a dish, then clean the fish as usual.

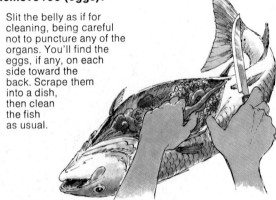

Skin eel:

Hang the eel at eye level and cut just through the skin 2″ or 3″ below the head. Grip the skin . . .

tightly and pull down hard. The skin will pull off just like taking off a stocking.

Fillet:

You need not clean or scale the fish. Cut along the back from tail to head;

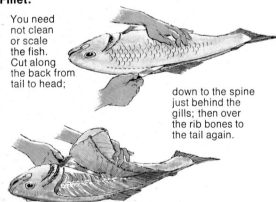

down to the spine just behind the gills; then over the rib bones to the tail again.

Lift the fillet free in one piece; turn the fish over and do the same on the other side.

Skin the fillet:

Lay the fillet flat and peel the skin up on one end. Grip the skin tightly and slide the knife between the skin and the meat.

---

5. Sprinkle another third of the dill with the cognac on the upturned fillet and cover it with the other fillet, making a sandwich, resembling a section of the whole fish.

6. Cover the fish with the remaining dill and twigs, and press it down with a weighted board.

7. Let stand for 2 days in a cool place and then refrigerate. To serve, scrape off the fish and slice it very thin. Garnish with more dill, lemon, and mustard sauce. This fish will keep for 1 week in the refrigerator. (Makes 16 entrée servings or 32 appetizers)

Alaskan Pickled Salmon

Salmon filets, cut into small pieces
1 cup water
1 cup distilled white vinegar
3 tablespoons sugar
1 lemon, sliced
1 onion, sliced
1 tablespoon mixed pickling spice

1. Spread fish in shallow glass pan.

2. Combine remaining ingredients, bring to a boil, let cool and pour over fish. Refrigerate. Can be eaten after 24 hours, but flavor improves after several days. (Will pickle 8 or 9 pints)

Caviar

1 gallon water
2½ cups salt (or more)
⅛ ounce sodium nitrate (saltpeter), available from druggist
1/32 ounce sodium nitrite
1 teaspoon *each* powdered ginger and dry mustard
Eggs, from sturgeon, northern pike, crappie, bluegill, perch, walleye, or carp

1. Combine water and salt to form a density that an egg will float on.

2. Add remaining ingredients except fish eggs.

3. Remove egg sack from fish. (If using carp, discard meat, other fish can be used for dinner.) Squeeze eggs into solution. Let stand for five days at room temperature.

4. Strain eggs from curing solution. Place in clean sterile glass jars. Seal. Keep refrigerated.

Note: Check with your local fish-market and ask them to secure one of the above kinds of female fish for making caviar. The best sturgeon come from the Mississippi River around Winona, Minnesota.

Pickled salmon is a visual treat as well as a delight to the taste buds.

Ways to use pickled vegetables and fruits

PICKLES-RELISHES CATSUPS-CHUTNEYS CONDIMENTS & SAUCES	APPETIZERS				EXOTICA					SALADS					FISH					MEATS					
	first courses	with cocktails	picnics-barbeques	antipasto	Latin & Spanish cuisine	Jewish delicatessen	mid-eastern dishes	oriental dishes	curries	fruit salads	meat salads	fish salads	tossed-mixed salads	green salads	shell-fish composed dishes	fried fish	broiled fish	poached fish	smoked fish	hamburger	beef roast	pork & lamb	steaks & chops	roast fowl	cold cuts
pickled artichokes		●						○																	●
pickled asparagus	●																			○					●
pickled string beans		●	●	○		○													○						●
marinated legumes	●		●				○									○				●		●			●
Mississippi relish			●			○															●	●		●	
pickled beets		●									●		●							●				●	●
russel & borsht	●					●											○	●							
pickled broccoli		●						○					○												
pickled Brussels sprouts		●																	○						●
pickled cabbage			●					○														●			
sauerkraut		●				●					●									●	●				●
pickled carrots		●																					●		
cauliflower pickles		●	●				○						●		○					●					●
corn relish		●														●									●
celery relish		●																							●
miniature corn, carrots, etc.	●												●												
dilled cucumber pickles		●	●			○									○	●				●		●			●
sweet cucumber pickles		●	●			○							○							●		●			●
spicy (mustard, garlic) cucumber pickles			●												○					●		●			●
eggplants																									
babu-ganouj & eggplant caviar	●	●		○			○																		
oriental salted pickles	●							○	●																
horseradish						○					●							●			●	●			○
pickled mushrooms	●	●	●					○															●	●	●
artichoke relish		●														●				●					
pickled okra		●	●		●			○																	
olives	●	●	●	●	●	●	●		●		●	●								●		●			●
pickled onions		●	●										●							●					●
onion relishes		●														●				●					●
sweet & sour sauce							○									●						●		●	
sweet pickled peppers		●	●		●				○		●									●					●
hot pickled peppers	●	●	●	●				○												●					●
pepper relishes		●			●															●					
hot sauces					●		●	●													●	●			
radish relishes		●				○														●	●				
rhubarb relish																●									●
pickled zucchini		●	●	●				○											○	●					●
zucchini relishes		●																		●					●
pickled pumpkin		●	●																	●					
pickled tomatoes	●	●	●	●		○										●				●					●
tomato relishes		●																		●					●
tomato sauces (catsups)		●				○														●			●		●
pickled turnips		●					○	●					●										●		●
hot chutneys & relishes		●							●							●				●	●	●		●	
sweet chutneys & relishes		●							●							●	●			●		●		●	
pickled bananas					●																			●	
spiced berries										●						●						●		●	
pickled cherries																								●	
melon pickles (& rinds)		●														●						●		●	
crabapple pickles & relish		●																		●		●		●	
pickled fruits		●								●						●				●		●		●	
sweet pickled fruits		●								●												●	●	●	
fruit relishes		●														●				●		●		●	
fruit catsups		●														●				●		●			●
spiced citrus fruits		●	●					○		●						●				●				●	○

● traditional accompaniment

○ not traditional, but delicious

Serving suggestions for pickled meat, fish and egg

PICKLED MEATS, FISH, AND EGGS	APPETIZERS & HORS D'OEUVRES	LUNCHEON ENTRÉES	DINNER ENTRÉES
Caviar	with toast or crackers, grated hard egg & onion.	in crepes with sour-cream garnish eggs a la Russe.	
Swedish Pickled Salmon	sliced very thin with butter on dark bread.	sliced thin with tomatoes, hard eggs and fresh dill.	
Poisson Cru	on a lettuce leaf with lime wedges.	with tomatoes, hard eggs in an avocado half, lime.	
Sweet & Sour Fish		with salads, green salad, mixed tossed salad and German potato salad or cabbage, white bread.	
Pickled Fish		dark bread and butter—salad, green or mixed—cold vinegared potatoes, vegetable vinaigrette.	
Pickled Shrimp	on lettuce with horse-radish sauce.	with tomatoes, hard eggs, greens, rolls and butter.	
Marinated Shrimp	on lettuce leaf with seasoned mayonnaise.	with tomato aspic, grated hard egg, avocado, asparagus.	
Pickled Oysters	on toothpicks with pickled vegetables.		
Seviche	on lettuce leaf.	with lettuce, hard egg slices, tomato wedges and avocado.	
Pickled Eel	on toothpicks with sweet pickles.		
Pickled Pike		with mixed tossed salads, slaw or vegetables, vinaigrette, stuffed mushrooms, white bread.	
Crock Pickled Sardines	with sliced red onion and lemon juice.	in sandwiches with onion, tomato, and mustard.	
Potted Herring		hot, with boiled buttered potatoes and carrots, salad, black bread & butter.	
Herring in Dark Wine	with lettuce and onion.		
Herring in Cream	with lettuce, onion and sour cream.		
Inlagd Sil	with hot boiled parsleyed potatoes, *aquavit*, beer, and white bread.		
Pickled Pigs Feet		with salad, black-eyed peas, collard greens, corn bread & butter.	
Sauerbraten			with dumplings or potatoes, red cabbage, pumpernickel.
Sweet and Sour Heart			with cabbage & apples, salad and rye bread.
Mincemeat		(for pies and plum puddings)	
Spiced Pickled Beef		with salads; potato or tossed; boiled, buttered vegetables, french bread.	
Corned Beef	make hash with onions and potatoes, serve on sesame crackers.	sandwiches on English muffins with melted cheese and Sauerkraut.	with boiled cabbage and potatoes.
Kosher Style Corned Beef		sandwiches on rye bread with mustard & pickles.	alone or with other cold cuts, slaw, pickles and potato salad.
Garlic Pickled Eggs	deviled on shredded lettuce.	with seasoned mayonnaise capers, and salad.	
Pickled Eggs with Beets	deviled with hot, sweet mustard and relish.	in egg salad with sweet relish and mustard.	
Spiced Pickled Eggs		with cold cuts, horseradish and mustard, tossed salad and dark bread.	
Pickled Chinese Tea Eggs	whole on lettuce with seasoned mayonnaise.		

Showing off

Anyone who's lived in a rural environment will know how much food competitions are a part of the county fair. Along with baking and canning, pickling is popular at the smallest church bazaar or the largest of the county and state fairs.

Pickle Competition

Good cooks might be interested in entering their wares in local competition. Win or lose it's a great way to meet other cooks, exchange ideas, and to improve your techniques. It's also a good way to learn just how super a cook you are, and it's the only competition known in which you can eat all the contestants.

Some contests are for judging the appearance of food only. Others judge appearance and taste.

Be sure to secure a copy of the rules. There will usually be different classes for the same foods, guidelines for jar types and sizes and requirements for information on the jars themselves.

The general standards by which pickled foods are judged are noted on our facsimile scorecard.

If you plan on entering food competitions you'll have to be meticulous at every stage of the pickling procedure. Food will have to be very fresh, home grown if possible. Vine-

Judge's score card—Pickling

Fruit Pickles		Maxi-mum Point
Appearance	texture, firmness, fullness	
	size, shape, uniformity	
	color of fruit	
	color of liquid	50
Flavor	spiciness, sweetness, sourness	40
Containers	uniformity, cleanliness labeling	10
Vegetable Pickles		
Appearance	texture, firmness, crispness	
	size, shape, uniformity	
	color of vegetable	
	color of liquid	50
Flavor	tartness, pungency	40
Containers	uniformity, cleanliness, labeling	10
Relishes		
Appearance	characteristic of ingredients	
	color	
	texture, firmness	
	uniformity of chopping	50
Flavor	seasoning sweetness, hotness	40
Containers	uniformity, cleanliness, labeling	10

gars will have to be clear, unclouded. None of the foods can be over or under cooked.

Don't rush any of your pickles to meet competition deadlines. Be sure that they're aged the proper time. You will be going up against the best of other good cooks, so there is very little room for error from the first selection of food to the final aging.

Write or call your County Farm or Home Adviser for the dates and addresses of local fairs and fair committees. Then write the fairs' offices and ask for a premium book. This book will provide all information relating to times, types of competition, rules, prizes and so on.

Giving pickles as gifts

As the planet shrinks and we draw, increasingly, upon its limited resources to feed ourselves, foods are seen as perfect gifts.

Pickled products are ideal, providing a sharpness of taste that is a refreshing relief from everyday foods. Pickles have a universal appeal but can also conform to the individual fruit or vegetable preference of the gift receiver.

Giving pickles as gifts also bespeaks an investment in time. Even quick-pickled products are aged for weeks at the minimum for maximum flavor. The gift of fermented pickles is one that results from months of work and cannot be duplicated by running out to the store.

Do the unusual. Pickle your friends' favorite berries and give them in the dead of winter. Pickle a pineapple and send it to someone in Hawaii. Take some pickled hot peppers to a Mexican dinner. An invitation to a barbecue can be appreciated by the gift of a homemade chutney or relish. Pickles can be individually seasoned for individual people. Remember that they can be made without salt and with sugar substitutes and can thus conform to anyone's specific dietary needs.

An assortment of pickles can be visually striking. Array green beans opposite tomatoes, or peaches opposite blueberries, in a box of two or three jars. A trio consisting of a fruit, a vegetable and a relish is a nice combination of contrasting tastes.

Those who receive pickled products as gifts are getting something unique. It's a personal gift, handmade and certainly one-of-a-kind.

A blue ribbon can be a compliment to the pickler's talents. Win or lose there's a lot to be gained from showing your product and sharing experiences with other cooks.

Gifts of pickled products can express your imagination and best wishes for any occasion.

Helpful hints

The language of pickles: guide to seasoning, weights, measurements and conversion charts; tips on fresh produce yields; recommended reading.

The language of pickles

Acid food. All fruits, tomatoes, ripe pimiento peppers, pickles, rhubarb and sauerkraut.

Acidity. The amount of acid naturally available in fresh produce, usually identified by a strong, biting taste.

Blanch. To scald or parboil in water or steam for whitening or to remove skin. Dipping immediately into cold water allows for easy handling.

Boiling. To heat water to the boiling point so that it bubbles and rolls from top to bottom and reaches a temperature of 212 degrees Fahrenheit or 100 degrees Centigrade at sea level.

Botulism. Acute, often deadly food poisoning caused by the presence of botulin toxin in food.

Bread and butter pickles. Made from fresh, green cucumbers by quick pasteurizing method. Mildly spiced, sweet, crosscut slices.

Brine. A solution of salt and water in which raw vegetables are immersed for long periods to cure.

Brine-cured. A vegetable sufficiently chemically changed by brine-soaking in order to be made long-lasting. Now ready to be made into various types of pickles.

Canner. A canning kettle for boiling-water bath or a pressure canner for processing foods at high temperatures.

Capers. Pickled flower buds of caper shrubs served as condiment. False capers are made from nasturtium buds.

Catsup. A seasoned condiment-sauce, usually made from tomatoes.

Chow-chow. Chopped mixed pickles in a mustard sauce.

Chutney. A highly seasoned sweet condiment of pickled fruits, herbs and spices.

Condiment. A pungent seasoning to enhance the flavor of other foods.

Crock. A thick eathernware pot or jar.

Crock pickles. Pickles that are kept stored in a crock, immersed in brine, rather than being canned in jars.

Cure. To prepare by chemical or physical processing for keeping or use.

Dill pickle. Strongly flavored with dill. Processed by lengthy natural fermentation or begun in brine and finished later in a dill solution.

Exhausting (venting). Allowing steam to escape from the steam valve of a pressure canner for a given time period. This forces the air from the cooker so that only live steam remains during processing.

Fermentation. A chemical process which is used to alter the organic compounds of certain foods for specific flavors. A classic example of a fermented food is sauerkraut.

Flowerets. Small flowers which comprise the flower heads of such vegetables as cauliflower and broccoli.

Freshening. Soaking brined vegetables in water or water and vinegar to remove excess salt before continuing the pickling process.

Gherkins. Small prickly cucumbers used for pickling.

Herbs. Non-woody plants valued for their fragrance and savory taste.

Headspace. Empty area between top of jar and the food. Usually ¼ to ½ inch between liquid and lid.

Hot pack. Food that has been pre-cooked and is hot when packed in jars.

Kosher. Food sanctioned by Hebrew law. In general usage the term refers to foods of the Jewish heritage.

Low acid foods. All vegetables, except tomatoes and ripe pimiento peppers, all meats.

Mustard pickles. Flavored with ground, dry mustard or whole mustard seed.

Marinade. A brine or pickling liquid in which vegetables or meats are soaked, usually overnight, to enrich the flavor and prolong keeping time.

Open kettle canning. Placing prepared foods directly into hot, sterile jars and covering immediately with sterile lid and ring. Not recommended.

Overnight. At least 12 hours.

Pack. Manner in which food is put in jars.

Pasteurize. Process of destroying bacteria by heating liquid to a temperature of 142-to-145 degrees Fahrenheit for 30 minutes.

Petcock. The steam valve of a pressure canner.

Piccalilli. Fine chopped sour pickles of one type or mixed fine-chopped sour vegetable picklets.

Pickle. Any food that has been preserved in brine or in vinegar.

Pickling spices. Many commercial blends of spices for pickling are available. Usually made from a mixture of allspice, bay leaves, black peppercorns, cardamon, cinnamon sticks, cloves, coriander seed, dill seed, ginger, mace, mustard seed and red peppers.

Polish dills. Fresh cucumbers canned in a dill solution resulting in a flavor combination of the fresh vegetable and dill.

Precooking. Cooking in simmering or boiling liquid or over steam for a given time period before packing in jars for processing.

Preserving agents. Ingredients used in pickling processes—vinegar, salt, sugar—to prolong keeping time of produce.

Pressure canner. A covered cooker with a pressure gauge or thermometer on top; allows higher temperatures than open kettles can reach to assure destruction of any bacteria in canned foods.

Processing. Cooking food after it has been placed in the storage container either by boiling-water bath or pressure canner.

Quickles. Pickles made from fresh vegetables by quick processing methods rather than long fermentation.

Relish. A condiment of fine-chopped vegetables, fruits, or combinations, usually highly spiced.

Russel. Fermented beet juice.

Salsa. Mexican relish of tomatoes, onion and peppers.

Salt. Oldest preservative. Brings out natural flavor of foods. In addition to tablesalt (sodium chloride), there are mixed herb salts and a variety of seasoned forms.

Salting. Preserving process of curing vegetables by packing in salt to form brine.

Scalding. A heating process which raises the temperature of a liquid just below the boiling point. Used often to remove the skins of vegetables and fruits.

Sealing. Securing container lids to keep bacteria and air from entering.

Simmering. Cooking at a constant heat just under the boiling point.

Sour pickles. Brine-cured pickles finished in sour vinegar with spices and herbs.

Spices. Aromatic vegetable products used to season or flavor foods.

Steeping. A soaking process used to soften, cleanse, or extract some constituent.

Sterilize. To make free of microorganisms. This can be achieved by boiling

steadily in water for at least 15 minutes.

Sweet pickles. Brine-cured pickles finished in sweet liquids of varying degrees to which spices have been added.

Vinegar. Sour liquid containing acetic acid, obtained by fermentation of dilute alcoholic liquids. Used as a condiment or preservative.

Water bath. A process in which canned foods are immersed in boiling water for a specified time to kill any unwanted bacteria.

Sweetener yield

Sweetener, per pound	Yield
Honey, strained	1½ cups
Molasses	1½ cups
Sugar, brown	2 cups, packed
Sugar, cane	1½ cups
Sugar, confectioner's	2½ to 3 cups
Sugar, fruit	2¼ cups
Sugar, granulated	2 cups

Metric conversion

Common prefixes (to be used with basic units)	
Milli:	one-thousandth (0.001)
Centi:	one-hundredth (0.01)
Deci:	one-tenth (0.1)
Decka:	ten times (10)
Hecto:	one-hundred times (100)
Kilo:	one-thousand times (1000)

Common units of volume

Unit	Metric System	Avoirdupois System
1 teaspoon	5.0 milliliters	60 drops
1 tablespoon	15.0 milliliters	3 teaspoons or ½ fluid ounce
1 fluid ounce	30.0 milliliters	2 tablespoons
1 cup	0.24 liter	8 fluid ounces or 16 tablespoons
1 pint	0.47 liter	2 cups
1 quart (liquid)	0.95 liter	2 pints
1 gallon (liquid)	0.004 cubic meter	4 quarts
1 peck	0.009 cubic meter	8 quarts
1 bushel	0.04 cubic meter	4 pecks

Common units of weight

Unit	Metric System	Avoirdupois System
1 gram		0.035 ounces
1 kilogram	1000 grams	2.21 pounds
1 ounce	28.35 grams	
1 pound	453.59 grams	16 ounces

Nutritive analysis of pickles

The composition of 100 grams of edible portion (approx. 1 large dill pickle or ½ cup of fresh cucumber pickle slices) is listed below:

	Fermented Dill Pickles		Sweet Pickles		Sour Pickles		Fresh Pack Cucumber Pickles	
Water	93.3%		60.7%		94.8%		78.7%	
Food Energy	11	calories	146	calories	10	calories	73	calories
Protein	.7	gm.	.7	gm.	.5	gm.	0.9	gm.
Fat	.2	gm.	.4	gm.	.2	gm.	.2	gm.
Carbohydrate	2.2	gms.	36.5	gms.	2.0	gms.	17.9	gms.
Ash	3.6	gms.	1.7	gms.	2.5	gms.	2.3	gms.
Calcium	26.0	mgs.	12.0	mgs.	17.0	mgs.	32.0	mgs.
Iron	1.0	mg.	1.2	mg.	3.2	mgs.	1.8	mgs.
Vitamin A	100	I.U.	90	I.U.	100	I.U.	140	I.U.
Thiamine		trace		trace		trace		trace
Riboflavin	.02	mg.	.02	mg.	.02	mg.	.03	mg.
Vitamin C	6.0	mgs.	6.0	mgs.	7.0	mgs.	9.0	mgs.
Phosphorus	21.0	mgs.	16.0	mgs.	15.0	mgs.	27.0	mgs.
Potassium	200.0	mgs.	—		—		—	
Sodium	1428.0	mgs.	—		1353.0	mgs.	673.0	mgs.

Guide to pickling seasonings

Seasoning	Type	Form	Description	Uses
Allspice	Spice	Whole or ground berries	Natural blend of the flavors of cloves, cinnamon and nutmeg	Fruit, meat and sweet pickles; chutneys, catsups, vinegars
Anise	Herb	Seed, fresh or dried leaves	Sweet, spicy, licorice taste and fragrance	Sweet pickles, chutneys
Basil	Herb	Fresh or dried leaves and tender stems	Very fragrant and spicy taste	Mustard pickles, vinegars, relishes, catsups
Bay	Spice	Dried leaves	Strong pungent smell, almost bitter taste	Vegetable pickles and relishes, vinegars, meat pickling liquid
Borage	Herb	Fresh or dried leaves and flowers	Fresh cucumber flavor	Vinegars, relishes
Bouquet garni	Herbs	Fresh or dried sprigs	Mixed herbs for desired taste, tied together while cooking	Vinegars, catsups, chutneys
Burnet	Herb	Fresh or dried leaves	Delicate cucumber-like flavor	Marinated salads and fish, vinegar
Caraway	Herb	Seed or fresh leaves and root	Spicy, aromatic seed; sweet, delicate leaves and root	Cabbage pickles, sauerkraut, sweet pickles
Cardamon	Herb	Whole or ground seed	Pleasant, pungent aroma and taste	Sweet pickles, relishes, chutneys
Cayenne	Spice	Dried whole pod or ground	Very hot red pepper	Catsups, relishes
Celery	Vegetable	Fresh or dried leaves, fresh stalk or roots, dried seed	Delicately flavored	Relishes, vegetable pickles, marinades, catsups
Chervil	Herb	Fresh or dried leaves	Delicately flavored, parsley-like	Catsups, vegetable pickles, relishes
Chili powder	Spice	Powder	Hot or mild peppery taste	Relishes, tomato pickles, catsups, mustard pickles
Chives	Herb	Fresh leaves or bulbs	Delicate onion flavor	Pickled bulbs, relishes
Cinnamon	Spice	Ground or stick	Aromatic bark, varying in pungent taste	Chutneys, catsups, vinegars, pickled fruits and vegetables
Cloves	Spice	Whole or ground buds	Very aromatic, warm, spicy taste	Spiced fruits, vinegars, sweet pickles, pickled meats
Coriander	Herb	Whole or ground seed	Similar to orange or lemon peel in flavor	Vinegars, sweet pickles; anything containing cabbage.
Creole pepper	Vegetable	Dried pods or ground, or liquid form	Very hot, similar to cayenne	Catsups, hot relishes
Cress	Herb	Fresh leaves	Spicy, peppery taste	Relishes, sweet pickles, vinegars
Cumin	Herb	Whole or ground seed	Very aromatic with bitterish flavor	Ingredient of curry powder, relishes and vinegar
Curry powder	Spices and herbs	Combination of powders or blended paste	Pungent aroma; mild to extremely hot depending on mixture of ingredients	Mustard pickles, vinegar
Dill	Herb	Fresh leaves, fresh or dried flowers, seed	Pungent aroma and flavor	Pickles, sauerkraut, relish, vinegars
Fennel	Herb	Fresh and dried leaves, stalk and seed	Licorice taste	Sweet pickles, sauerkraut, catsup, spiced fruit
Fenugreek	Herb	Seed	Bitter taste and aromatic smell	Chutneys, especially mango
Garlic	Bulb	Dried, powdered, salt, oil	Pungent aroma and flavor	Kosher and Polish pickles, relishes, vinegar, meat pickles
Geranium	Herb	Fresh and dried leaves	Variety of delicious aromas and flavors (apple, lemon, nutmeg, mint, rose)	Relishes, pickles, chutneys, vinegars
Ginger	Herb	Dried whole or ground root, or crystallized	Sweet, spicy and highly aromatic	Pickles, chutneys, spiced fruits
Horse-radish	Herb	Fresh root or powdered dry root	Very pungent aroma, hot taste	Vinegar, mustard pickles, relishes
Juniper berry	Fruit	Dried berries	Slightly bittersweet, spicy aroma	Vinegars, sauerkraut, pickled meats and fish, relishes
Leek	Herb	Fresh bulb or stalks	Fragrant with mild onion taste	Relishes, catsups, vinegars

Seasoning	Type	Form	Description	Uses
Lemon	Fruit	Juice, rind, or oil	Tart aroma and flavor	Use as partial substitute for vinegar, fruit pickles, chutneys
Lime	Fruit	Juice, rind, or oil	Aromatic and tart, not as sweet as lemon	Chutney, fruit pickles, pickled fish
Mace	Spice	Flakes or ground dried layer between husk and kernel of nutmeg	Similar, but stronger flavor of nutmeg	Chutneys, spiced fruits, vinegars
Marjoram	Herb	Fresh, whole, crushed, or dry leaves	Spicy fragrance, warm flavor	Mustard pickles, relishes, vinegars
Mint	Herb	Fresh or dried leaves	Variety of flavors, highly fragrant	Chutneys, spiced fruits, vinegars
Mustard	Herb, spice	Fresh leaves, seed, powder, or condiment	Great variety of sharp flavors	Mustard pickles, vinegars, mixed vegetable pickles, catsups, relishes
Myrtle	Shrub	Fresh or dried leaves or seed	Highly aromatic, slightly bitter	Substitute for bay leaves
Nasturtium	Flower	Flowers, leaves, or seed pods	Similar to water cress in flavor	Pickle seed pods as capers, vinegars, relishes, marinades
Nutmeg	Spice	Whole dried kernel or ground	Strong spicy fragrance, bitterish	Chutneys, spiced fruits, relishes, pickles
Onion	Bulb	Fresh, dried, powder, or juice	Ranges from delicate to hot flavor	Pickles, relishes, vinegars, chutneys, catsups, sauerkraut, pickled meats
Oregano	Herb	Fresh or dried leaves	Pungent flavor and aroma	Mustard pickles, relishes, catsups, vinegars
Paprika	Vegetable	Ground pods and seed of sweet red peppers	Pungent and sweet	Mild flavor and color in pickles and relishes
Parsley	Herb	Fresh or dried leaves	Delicate flavor, rich in vitamins	Catsups, relishes, vinegars, pickles
Pepper	Spice	Dried whole berries (peppercorns) or ground	White has milder taste, black very potent	Use white where light color should be maintained in pickling; use whole in vegetable and meat pickling
Rosemary	Herb	Fresh or dried leaves	Piny flavor with spicy aroma	Mustard pickles, vinegars, relishes, meat pickling
Saffron	Spice	Dried flower stigma	Almost bitter flavor, sweet aroma	Mustard or curry pickles, use for yellow coloring
Sage	Herb	Fresh or dried leaves	Highly pungent	Sparingly in meat pickling, mustard pickles, relishes
Savory	Herb	Fresh or dried leaves	Slight resin odor and thyme-like flavor	Mustard pickles, vinegars, meat pickling, relishes
Sesame seed	Herb	Dried seeds or oil	Similar flavor of almonds	Vegetable pickles
Shallot	Bulb	Fresh or dried	Strong, but mellow onion-like flavor	Pickles, relishes, vinegars
Soy sauce	Beans	Fermented juice of soybeans	Very salty, Chinese catsup	Relishes, Oriental pickling, catsups
Tabasco	Vegetable	Sauce of vinegar and small red peppers	Extremely hot	Catsups, relishes, hot pickles, meat pickling
Tarragon	Herb	Fresh and dried leaves and flower tops	Sweet flavor and highly aromatic	Vinegars, catsups, vegetable pickles, chutneys, meat pickling
Thyme	Herb	Fresh or dried leaves	Pungent fragrance. Some varieties with lemon, orange, or caraway flavor	Vinegars, mustard pickles
Turmeric	Spice	Ground or whole root	Mild, warm flavor, yellow color	Mustard or yellow vegetable pickles, chutneys, good substitute for saffron
Vanilla	Spice	Stick or extract in alcohol	Sweet aroma and flavor	Chutney, spiced fruits
Verbena	Herb	Fresh or dried leaves	Lime or lemon flavor	Vinegar, relishes, sweet pickles
Watercress	Herb	Fresh leaves and stems	Peppery, pungent flavor and aroma	Marinades, vinegars
Wine	Fruits	Fermented juice	Complete range of flavors and colors	Vinegars (except sweet wines), Marinades, Burgundy and claret best for pickling meats

Fresh produce yield

Produce	Weight	Quantity	Yield
Almonds	3½ pounds	100 unshelled	4½ cups
Apples	1 pound 48-50 pounds	6 medium 1 bushel	3 cups chopped 20 quarts chopped
Apricots	1 pound	8-14 medium	3 cups whole 2 cups halved
Bananas	1 pound	3 medium	1¼ cups mashed 2-2½ cups sliced
Beans, green	1 pound	3-4 cups	2⅔-3 3/5 cups snapped for cut
Beets	1 pound	4-6 medium	3½ cups cooked, diced
Broccoli	1½-2½ pounds	1 bunch	4-4½ cups chopped
Brussels sprouts	1 pound	15-20 sprouts	3½ cups
Cabbage	2 pounds	1 head	7-8 cups shredded 3 cups cooked
Carrots	1 pound	4 large	2½ cups sliced or diced 3 cups chopped, cooked
Cauliflower	1½ pounds	1 head	4 cups flowerets
Celery	1 pound	8-12 stalks	4 cups diced
Cherries	1 pound	3 cups	2½ cups pitted
Corn	12-18 pounds	16-20 ears	2 quarts cut
Cranberries	1 pound	4-6 cups	2-2½ cups ground
Cucumbers	1 pound 6 pounds 6 pounds 9-12 pounds	2 large 100 very small 50 medium 50 3- to 4-inch	2 cups sliced 1 gallon whole 1 gallon whole 6-8 quarts whole
Currants	1 pound	2⅔ cups	2-2½ cups
Figs	1 pound	12-18 medium	2½-3 cups chopped
Gooseberries	1 pound	2⅔ cups	2⅔ cups
Grapefruit	1¼ pounds	1 large	1¾ cups broken 10-12 sections
Grapes	1 pound	2⅔ cups	2 cups halved 1 cup purée
Lemons	4 pounds	12 large	2½ cups juice 12 teaspoons grated rind
Lima beans	1 pound	100 pods	2-3 cups shelled
Limes	2¾ pounds	12 medium	1½-2 cups juice
Mangoes	1 pound	2-4	2 cups peeled, sliced
Mushrooms	1 pound	2½ cups	1½ cups sliced
Muskmelons	2 pounds	1 medium	1 cup chopped
Nectarines	1 pound	3-5 medium	2 cups peeled and sliced
Olives	1 pound	135 "small" 70 "mammoth" 40 "colossal" 32 "super colossal"	Same Same Same Same
Onions	1 pound	3 large or 4-4½ medium	2-2½ cups diced 2 cups chopped or ground
Oranges	6 pounds	12 medium	3-5 cups juice 6 cups diced
Peaches	1 pound 48 pounds	3-5 medium 1 bushel	2-2½ cups peeled, sliced 18-24 quarts, peeled
Pears	1 pound 48-50 pounds	4-5 medium 1 bushel	2⅔ cups peeled, sliced 20-25 quarts
Pecans	2½ pounds	75 unshelled	3 cups, halved
Peppers	1 pound	4 large	2 cups trimmed or chopped
Pineapple	3 pounds	1 medium	3-3½ cups peeled, diced
Plums	1 pound 50-56 pounds	12-20 medium 1 bushel	2 cups sliced 24-30 quarts
Prunes (dried)	1 pound	30-40 medium	4 cups cooked 2½ cups cooked, chopped
Raisins (seedless)	1 pound	3 cups	2½ cups chopped
Raisins (seeded)	1 pound	2½ cups	2 cups chopped
Strawberries	1 quart	3 cups	1 pint crushed 1 1/5 cups purée
Squash	2¼ pounds	12 medium	6 cups ground
Tomatoes	1 pound 8 pounds 53 pounds	4 medium 32 medium 1 bushel	3 cups sliced 4 quarts peeled, sliced 15-20 quarts
Turnips	1 pound	3-4 medium	3½-4½ sliced
Walnuts (English)	2½ pounds	50 unshelled	4 cups halved
Watermelon	30 pounds	10 pounds rind	3¼-4 quarts chopped
Zucchini	1 pound	3 medium	2¼ cups sliced

Recommended reading

✓A PRIMER FOR PICKLES, A READER FOR RELISHES: Ruby Stark Gutherie and Jack Stark Gutherie, 101 Productions.

✓BALL BLUE BOOK: Ball Brothers, Incorporated, Muncie, Indiana.

✓BERNARDIN HOME CANNING GUIDE: Bernardine, Incorporated, Evansville, Ind.

✓BULL COOK AND AUTHENTIC HISTORICAL RECIPES AND PRACTICES: George Leonard Herter and Berthe E. Herter, Herters, Waseca, MN 56093.

✓COMPLETE GUIDE TO HOME CANNING, PRESERVING AND FREEZING, USDA: direct reprints of several of the best publications from the USDA. Send $2.50 to 180 Varick Street, New York, NY 10014.

✓FREEZING AND CANNING COOKBOOK: Farm Journal, edited by Nell B. Nichols.

✓KERR CANNING BOOK: Kerr Glass Company, Sand Springs, OK.

✓OLD TIME PICKLING AND SPICING RECIPES: Florence Brobeck, Gramercy Books.

✓PICKLES AND PRESERVES: Marian Brown, Funk and Wagnells.

✓PICKLES, RELISH AND CHUTNEY: Irena Chalmers, Potpourri Press.

✓PUTTING FOOD BY: Hertzberg, Vaughan, Greene, Steven Green Press.

✓PUTTING UP STUFF FOR THE COLD TIME: Crescent Dragonwagon, Workman Publishing.

✓STOCKING UP: Rodale Press.

✓THE COMPLETE BOOK OF PICKLES AND RELISHES: Leonard Louis Levinson, Hawthorn Books.

✓12 MONTHS HARVEST: Ortho Book Series.

✓WHEN THE GOOD COOK GARDENS: Ortho Book Series.

Bulletins on home canning and pickling are available from your state Cooperative Extension Service. Call or write in care of your state university.

USDA bulletins are listed in a catalogue (Number 0103-0002, 45¢) available from Superintendent of Documents, U.S. Government Printing Office, Washington, DC 30402.

Local information can be obtained through your County Extension Agent. See your phone book for listings of county departments—or under the name of the County Agent in your county.

Commercial pickle sizes

Name	Length (inches)	Count per quart
Midgets #1	1¼ to 2	162
Midgets #2	1¼ to 2	112
Midgets #3	1¼ to 2	85
Gherkins #1	2 to 2¾	65
Gherkins #2	2 to 2¾	56
Gherkins #3	2 to 2¾	40
Medium	3 to 4	10 to 30
Large	4 and over	3 to 10

Can sizes

No. 1 Can	1½ cups
No. 2 Can	2½ cups
No. 3 Can	4 cups
No. 10 Can	13 cups